SHAKEN BUT NOT STIRRED

SHAKEN BUT NOT STIRRED

My Story

Keith Chegwin

Hodder & Stoughton

British Library Cataloguing in Publication Data

Chegwin, Keith
Shaken But Not Stirred: My Story
I. Title
791.45092

ISBN 0 340 63978 4

Typeset by Phoenix Typesetting, Ilkley, West Yorkshire.

Printed and Bound in Great Britain by
Mackays of Chatham PLC, Chatham, Kent

Hodder and Stoughton
A Division of Hodder Headline PLC
338 Euston Road
London NW1 3BH

This book is dedicated to Maria Fielden, a friend indeed. Also to my dog Hollie who was always there. I love them both.

PREFACE

If you wanted to buy a book to learn more about cooking, you'd plump straight for an expert cook book written by a good old kitchen favourite like Delia Smith. Someone who's had years of experience and has obtained enough knowledge to write with confidence about the smallest detail in order that your sponge cakes rise every time. If you wanted to find out more about drink, then I would suggest buying a book from an equally knowledgeable expert, someone who's a professional pisshead, dipsomaniac, sot and drunk. It's taken some time to gain such extensive knowledge on what can only be described as a mysterious and taboo subject. In order to put this book together I've had to endure many years of heavy, laborious, strenuous, punishing, gruelling and taxing research. I bet David Attenborough never went to such great lengths to research his books.

I had to drink litres and litres of alcohol day in and day out just to get a taste for the subject. I had to learn how to sleep through the night in a pool of piss, hold back vomit in a friend's house till I made it to the loo, disguise the smell of drink on my breath using a Fisherman's Friend and perfect the art of being drunk whilst appearing to be sober. It was not easy.

There were various party games I learnt along the way, some of which amused me for hours. 'Hide the Bottle' was a cracker and, just like charades, each time you play it you have to be more inventive. 'Find the Bottle' was the toughest; I found it very time consuming. It is best played by someone with a photographic memory. There were physical skills I conquered after some trial and error and a lot of bruising: how to fall off a chair, out of a car, down stairs and off a stage were my best. Once again, they can only be grasped through time and experience and the latter can only be successfully accomplished if you're in a similar career to mine. The verbal exams I found the most difficult, and I failed dismally every time.

Overall, the judges' opinion of my drinking marathons was that I passed the exacting test with flying colours. Only through all my painstaking efforts with the volatile material I was working with did I become a bonafide, fully-fledged alcoholic. This being the case, I can now safely say I have gained enough expertise to write with confidence, a book on this fascinating subject.

Surprisingly, I managed to keep a diary throughout my drinking years and, through the scrawled writing, when I was so pissed that the pen ran off the page, I can just make out some of the things that happened to me. But the diaries weren't enough for me: the odd line that said 'Stayed in hotel for three days' really meant 'Drank so much that I couldn't get out of my hotel bed and had to stay three nights to sober up'. I wanted to write this book so that I could see the facts laid out in front of me.

Looking back, I have to smile at some of the unbelievable things I did in order to drink. I look at people sipping their pints or G and Ts at the end of a bar and wonder whether they, like me when I was drinking, have a packet of mints or some aftershave concealed about their person to hide the smell of drink. Or do they have a bottle of Eye Dew in a pocket to take away the redness in their blurry eyes? Whether, once they've had their fill, they'll go and find somewhere to sleep it off and make some implausible excuse for not going home that night? I also wonder how many people in this country would really like to stop drinking, but can't. Whether they, like me when I wanted to give up, just don't know where to start.

I decided to write a book about my drinking years so that every so often I could flick through its pages and remember that time in my life when I couldn't make it through the day without a bottle in my hand. Like remembering your childhood or school days, you tend to recollect only the good times. You forget about the times when you may have been victim of some awful prank by your best mate, when someone told lies about you and the days when you were shit scared to hand in your homework because you didn't have time to complete it or you hadn't understood it. I don't want to look back kindly on my drinking days. I need something tangible to grasp hold of at a moment's notice, so that I can quickly reflect on the horrific times they were.

At first when I thought about stopping, I tried to find some plain, simple information to help me decide first and foremost whether I had a problem and, if I had, what I could do about it. My only alternative was to seek some professional help, but at the time there was no way I was going to ask an outsider for assistance. I thought the easier option would be to obtain some literature and information about drinking so that, by gaining that knowledge, I might be able to do something about stopping. But my search was in vain.

This book is about how I struggled to give up drinking, and some of the events that happened along the way. It has not been easy for me to put the next chapters together, as writing has never been a strong point of mine. I've signed a lot of autographs and I've penned tons of letters of praise, as celebrities do, to television bosses about how wonderful their own programmes have been, but I've never written anything of length or substance before. Over the years I've successfully avoided writing and won't even let people see the notes I scribble to use for quick reference on television. I tend to use phonetics and I've been embarrassed on many an occasion when someone's glanced at them, especially the long words, as it looks like I can't spell. I've ended up being the butt of many a gag in the office.

This book is the story of my life with drink. There are bits of my life story in it, to fill in the odd gap, but I hasten to add that it's not an autobiography. Even I would be bored hearing about the twenty-seven years of my showbiz career. It's about a time in my life when alcohol took a hold and just wouldn't let go. How, over the years, I drank more and more and my life began to fall apart. How I spent a fortune on treatment for my addiction in some top clinics. How I took prescribed drugs and more to wean me off it. But none of these methods worked.

Eventually, after many trials and tribulations, I came to the conclusion the only way for me to stop was to do it on my own. It was me who had to make the decision of whether to live or die.

During my drinking, the people who were around me at the time had to put up with a hell of a lot. Late nights when I didn't come home and days when I just disappeared. They'd cover for me with untold lies about how I was ill and couldn't make it into work. If the phone rang they'd say I was out, when I was only feet away and unconscious. They had to cover for me whilst I was in clinics and apologise to friends and neighbours for my anti-social behaviour.

Witness to this was my ex-wife, Maggie Philbin. Like my close friends, she'd probably had more than enough by the time I stopped. Living with an alcoholic is not one of life's greatest pleasures.

Out of respect for her and concern for my daughter Rose's future, I've agreed not to talk about either of them in great depth. I have mentioned them as references during my story, because they were a part of my drinking, but it would be wrong for me to write about what they were going through, how they perceived me and what they were feeling. I can only speak for myself and what was happening to me at the time.

It's about how I, as an alcoholic, perceived those around me. Those mates who thought they could help and without realising it were really helping me to drink. I knew that if I ended up comatose on the kitchen floor a good buddy would come around, put poor little Keith to bed, clean him up and inadvertently set him up for another day of drinking. I'd wake up the following morning fresh as a daisy and start the same process all over again.

This is not just a book for drunks, though, it's also for the poor buggers who know or have to live with one.

By reading my story you may gain an insight into the insular world of the alcoholic. How the alcoholic promises never to touch a drop ever again and three months later, it's the same old story. How he or she vows not to go near the pub or into an off licence, and still end up getting pissed. This book may help you understand why alcoholics go to such great lengths to get a drink, how they're feeling and why time after time they, for some unknown reason, end up letting others down.

It would be very difficult for me to give advice to those people who come home every day to find their loved ones out cold and covered in vomit, lying on the sofa. I'm also aware that it's not easy to stand by and watch a family member or best mate go down the plug hole by drinking themselves into oblivion night after night. But reading my story may help you to understand a little bit.

I can tell you that it took more than just will-power to stop me drinking. Over the years, so many people suggested I just stop, take some control. Well, as far as I'm concerned, that's a bit like trying to take control when you've got a touch of the old Delhi belly, the shits. You try taking control when you're dying to cough but daren't. It would also be impossible for me to write a book which you could follow to the letter and hope to achieve the same result. Alcoholics are all so individual. If we were all alike, by now they would have probably brought out some wonder drug and none of us would have a problem – everything in life would be marvellous and none of this drinking business would ever have happened.

I don't profess to know the ins and outs of alcoholism, although there are some experts I came across who make loads of dosh by pretending they do. But the question I'm always asked is 'What is an alcoholic?' Well, from my own point of view, an alcoholic is not always the person who consumes tremendous amounts of booze. I have a best mate who even in my heyday could drink me under the table, but he was capable of keeping off the stuff for days after a heavy binge. Me, I couldn't keep off it. I drank all the time, morning, noon and night. I just couldn't stop. I found that alcohol became a problem when it started to affect my work and my social environment. I believe an alcoholic is a person who thinks more about drinking than anything else, someone whose whole life revolves around their next tipple. As soon as having a drink became more important to me than being with my family and friends, going to work, getting up in the morning, washing or even really wanting to live, in my view I became an alcoholic.

This is no casebook and I'm no Dr Finlay. I'm just writing about my own experiences and the way I tackled them. I got an awful lot of things wrong along the way, but I must have got some of them right.

CHAPTER ONE

It was the morning of *This Morning*. Only two people could save me now: Richard Madeley and Judy Finnigan. I don't know how I made it up to Granada telly land, but I remember struggling in some posh hotel to get washed and dressed and look a little more presentable for my début on Britain's most popular morning programme. What the hell was I doing? I was pissed and kept asking myself why I had been asked to go on the show. I'm no expert on household tips or gardening. I know nothing about cooking and I was certainly in no state to jump across Fred's weather map.

It was 5 November 1991 and well before eight in the morning. There seemed to be some urgency for me to get ready. A very nice lady, whom I presumed was from the production team, had given me a razor and some foam and was watching my every move. She must have known I was totally out of my tree. There I was, trying to have a shave like Rolf Harris doing one of his paintings, a bit here and a bit there, covered in blood and shaving foam. It looked like someone had hit me with a strawberry pavlova.

Experience told me that if I took my time it wouldn't be too long before I sobered up enough to make some sense of the predicament I was in. I finished my shave and looked desperately in the room for a change of clothes. Usually when I appear on television, I never wear the same outfit that I've travelled in. Shit, I couldn't find one. Nor could I find an overnight bag, a clothes holdall, or my toothbrush. I couldn't even remember travelling. How the hell had I got here?

The situation called for desperate measures and time didn't appear to be on my side. I wondered whether the hotel had a shop so I could buy something to wear. I even eyed up what the production lady was wearing. Luckily, I found my black polo neck on the floor but only found half of a black suit – thank God it was the trousers. To this day I still haven't found the jacket.

I looked more like the guy in the Milk Tray advert. If I'd had a rope I'd have absailed out of the bedroom window and gone home, although I don't think I would have got far in my current state. It was all I had, it would have to do.

I was ushered out of the room and into the hotel lift. I felt a bit like a pop star on his way on stage. I was aware that the people with me didn't want to let me out of their sight and it also appeared that they didn't want to let anyone else get too close.

As I was escorted to a waiting car, my mind ticked away like a 125 train. I sat in the back seat as the car sped through the quiet streets of Liverpool. Somewhere along the line, I remembered agreeing to be on the show to talk about stress and the pressures of living life in the fast lane that had led to my seeking medical help in a clinic. As the car got closer to the studio I did a bit of a Miss Marple, some detective work to try and glean more info. As the conversation developed, I was made aware that I wasn't there to talk about stress, but about drinking. I casually chatted and smiled in Cheggers style to the researcher, but inside I was in such a mess.

I can only assume that during one of my heavy drinking bouts she must have phoned for a chinwag and to go over some notes. Whilst pissed, I must have gone into one of my drink-a-log routines, told her about my problem and agreed to go on telly to talk about my addiction to drink and how I'd given up. Yet again, the amber nectar had got me into one bloody great mess.

I caught sight of myself in the rear-view mirror of the car. My eyes were like glowing charcoals, my face was bloated and I was sweating. I looked like one of those nutters who agree to run the London Marathon as a bet and only start training the night before. I certainly didn't look like someone who'd just given up drinking. I must have stunk of booze and heaven knows what the production team on the show thought of me as I staggered through a line of cameras in the studios at Albert Dock. I'd come in to talk about how I'd stopped drinking and here I was all blurry-eyed and looking ready for another.

I was shown into a hospitality room and got stuck into a jug of percolated coffee. One snippet of information I learnt whilst in a clinic was that if you've been drinking alcohol it's not a good idea to drink coffee. The caffeine hypes up the system, makes the blood in your body flow more quickly and for a short period you're on a high again. However, I found that it took away the shaking and dry vomiting for a short period. I already sensed that my body was about to start shaking and my stomach felt as if Chris Eubank had used it as a punch bag, so for me, at that time, coffee was the only way to get myself in shape. I drunk them dry and could feel myself slowly coming round, back on a high, which eased all my uncontrollable ailments.

I kept making space for myself by taking long visits to the loo and contemplating the absurd scenario. I'd really cocked it up this time. I looked at the running order for the show and saw that I was to be their main topic for debate. They'd even brought in some bleedin' expert to talk about controlled drinking and there was to be a phone-in for the viewers to ask questions. Oh dear!

I had to make a decision. I could either walk away, let them down and have the press knocking on my door enquiring why there was a huge gap in the programme and why I hadn't been there to fill it. Or, maybe, I should just go on and do it. If I told the whole world and his wife that I had a drink problem in the morning, I couldn't exactly pop into the off licence in the afternoon for fear of being spotted by a viewer or snapped by a photographer.

I was in a bloody mess with only an hour and a half to go before the show started. What should I do?

I went to the loo and sat in a cubicle rehearsing what I would say to Richard and Judy. I had one ear open just in case someone came in and heard my practising. No way could I go on air and tell them that my last drink was only a couple of hours before the programme started. I had to make up a story. I thought it best, for the short term, to tell the viewers, some of whom may have a drink problem themselves, that I was a recovering alcoholic, that I was going through a rough patch and that I had decided to give myself a couple of months' sobriety. It wasn't honest but it was the best I could come up with. It would at least get the national press, who'd been after me for some time, off my back.

Quite a few of the newspapers had threatened to run stories about me having a drink problem. I'd been into a clinic three times and they were very suspicious. I'd told them on each occasion that I was receiving treatment for stress. There are only so many times you can use an excuse like that and hope to get away with it. I'd had more stress than London's Tower Bridge.

There was one particularly persistent freelance journalist who was always knocking at my front door. He was the lowest of the low. At least the national journalists you can credit with some respect, no matter how annoying their harassing questioning might be. This man would grab any line of casual conversation and use it to write a story, make money for his company and presumably another clipping for his tacky portfolio. He'd walk up to my house or hang over my garden wall like a long lost relative. He was a pathetic Alan Bleasdale character: greasy hair, crumpled suit and thin, ill-fitting tie. He always had a notepad and pencil in hand and once I noticed there was a small cassette player concealed and whirring away in his inside jacket pocket. I wasn't sure whether he used it for reference or whether he played it to himself in bed at night or to his mates in the pub. He was the poor man's Roger Cook, a sad and pitiful person who made money from others like myself who were going through a bad patch.

I thought about him before I made my decision to go on the programme. I decided it was time to get it all out of the way. I'd had enough of hiding my drink. If I was to let people know that I was having a problem I would be one step ahead of the media. With such heavy drinking it wouldn't be too long before some eager newshound snapped me pissed at a party or found me comatose in my drive.

I was surprised they hadn't been tipped off about my drinking long before now. People in the area where I lived must have known I had a drink problem, but were kind enough to say nothing about my antics. I believe one of my neighbours found me curled up on his lawn and was good enough to take me home. They must have seen me staggering up and down the country lanes or coming out of the local shop weighed down by bottles of booze.

There was an occasion when hundreds of people were witness to my appalling behaviour and must have known I was drunk. I was invited one evening to act as auctioneer at a Rotary Club ball. I arrived in my dinner jacket and joined the rest of the fundraisers for pre-dinner drinkiepoos. I was offered a glass of champagne and took it. Bad move. I'd been hitting the bottle most of the day and I should have known better. On occasions when I've mixed my drinks I've always ended up in some kind of trouble. More than a few glasses of champers later, I sat down at my table and got stuck into the red and white wine. The other nine people about me seemed to be content with their soft drinks and dinner party chat. By the time the first course arrived I'd polished off a couple of bottles of wine and set about ordering some more, just in case someone else at the table wanted a glass.

Eventually, the first course arrived. I just about remember it was some kind of soup. I'm not sure whether I finished it or not as at some point I must have blacked out. The next thing I knew I was waking up in one of the hotel bedrooms being comforted by a local newspaper friend. He told me how people at the function were somewhat surprised that I hadn't made it to the main course and were curious to know why I had landed head first into my soup and then was carried out of the room by four Rotarians.

Although he was a newspaper man, for the first time ever I came straight out with it and told him I had a problem with drink. My honesty must have convinced him to tell the Rotary folk that I was a little unwell and had been working long hours, hence the strange behaviour. He gave me an hour to get my act together and told me that the only way this wasn't going to end up in the newspapers was for me to get back to the dinner table as quickly as possible and blame it all on exhaustion.

He left me for an hour to sleep it off and then helped me back to the awaiting guests. I sat with him at his table. By the time I'd returned to the party the rest of the dinner guests were all up and dancing and had had quite a few drinks themselves. I was lucky as I blended in with the rest of them and the whole event seemed to be forgotten.

Now there were about forty minutes to go. I saw Richard and Judy going over a few notes together. I was making conversation with people but I wasn't really all there. I was in such a dilemma. It was time to be open and honest about my problem, tell my side of the story rather than let it become gossip or malicious rumour in the newspapers which I would probably end up fighting for the rest of my life.

Once again, I needed some more time on my own, so I made my excuses and headed for the loo again. I came to the decision that this was it, I'd had my last drink. I'd drunk so many years away and I had desperately tried to give up so many times and in so many ways, but each time I'd failed. I knew deep down that the only way I was ever going to kick the habit was to get my act together, wipe the slate clean and start afresh.

Because drinking had always been the easier option, I had never had the nerve to be honest with either myself or those around me. Underneath it all, I'd always wanted the whole world to sod off for a while and leave me alone to get on with my life. I was getting so fed up with hearing about other people's problems and how they'd won their battles against booze. I was fed up with friends and family giving me advice and trying to help me, however good their intentions. I just couldn't take any more. I was bored with hearing about alternative treatments, acupuncture, hypnosis, counselling, therapy, clinics, doctors, drugs and holidays. I knew that if I could just have some breathing space there was a possibility I could give up on my own. I'd never had the chance.

I also knew that by disclosing my addiction on national TV I would inherit a whole new set of problems. For a start, there would be the embarrassment of everyone in the country knowing I was a drunk. If they didn't catch me on the programme that morning, I'm sure my Wapping friends would fill 'em in the following day. I reckoned I could handle the press, though: I'd give them the full story free of charge and then tell them to bugger off.

One of my most worrying concerns was the phone calls from everyone in my filofax that I hadn't spoken to for years. Most showbiz types only return your calls if you've been on the television the night before. If there was some national press coverage to be had though, they would appear like flies on horse shit, hoping for at least a name check. I could always put the answerphone on and monitor their calls.

I wondered how my family would cope. I knew I'd already put them, and a lot of other people, through quite a horrendous time but I was confident that I'd have their support. I was sure they wouldn't mind leaving me alone for a while if I made it clear to them what the outcome might be.

Weighing up all the odds, it was a chance I had to take and, bizarre as it may sound, this seemed the perfect opportunity to do just that. Telling people I was an alcoholic wasn't going to make me flavour of the month, but it was an honest start and this time, I thought, it might work.

I headed back to hospitality and more coffee. I was content to go ahead with the show. For a moment I wondered about my future prospects. My whole life had been in entertainment; for twenty-seven years I'd known nothing else. Some folk in the entertainment world rightly wouldn't be so keen to book a drunk to present a children's television series. I didn't think the top advertising agency Saatchi & Saatchi would be phoning up to ask me to appear in their new lager advert or promote the latest car. I knew it was going to take some time for people to trust me again. For them, it would be like getting on a plane and being told whilst taxi-ing to the runway that the pilot had a drink problem. I certainly would have thought twice about getting on for fear of him helping himself to more than his quota of duty frees whilst flying. This time I came to the conclusion that, whatever the outcome, I had to do it for me. It was time to get myself right and worry about the rest later.

I took a deep breath and looked round the studio set in the heart of Liverpool's docklands, now one of the city's trendiest areas. Then I cast my mind back to the days when I was a kid and my dad used to bring me down to the dockside to buy fresh fish off the small trawlers moored there . . .

CHAPTER TWO

I was born in Liverpool on 17 January 1957, twenty minutes after my identical twin brother Jeff. Only recently did I find out from my mother that it was touch and go at first whether I would survive. I was put in an incubator and left to struggle. Much to the relief of all concerned, I managed to pull through. In my youth I'd often brag to my mates that I was born in Walton Hospital, the same one as Paul McCartney. I have often wondered whether my hospital buddy Paul used the same story at dinner parties.

At this time Mum and Dad were living in rooms in Bootle with my sister Janice who was two years older than us. I believe they had had a pretty tough time of it and were obviously keen to move to somewhere bigger. They eventually got their ideal home: a three-bedroomed council house about a mile up the road.

Thirty-seven Aintree Road was Mum and Dad's pride and joy. It wasn't long after moving in that they had the opportunity to buy the place. Dad couldn't wait to get his hands on it – he was an incredible DIY enthusiast and was continuously knocking down walls here, panelling there and extending everywhere. Some days when I left for school I'd have a final look round. He'd made so many changes to the place that one day I was convinced I'd leave a three up two down in the morning and come home to find a one up one down with a sea view. Dad worked all hours for a timber merchant on the dock road, whilst Mum worked three days a week in the shoe department of a big shop in the city centre. We'd sometimes go and pick her up from work. That was after Dad made sure all three of us had cleaned the house from top to bottom. I'd do the hoovering whilst Jeff polished and Janice cleared up the kitchen. Dad supervised and occasionally mucked in.

Money was short but Mum and Dad left us asking for nowt. Only now do I really appreciate how hard they had to work to keep three kids up and running. I had a great childhood, although I didn't really enjoy my days at school. Jeff was the clever twin.

He was academically sound and very much into sport. He had a natural flair for football, although his style was more in tune with Vinny Jones and he was always being ticked off for it. He was regularly chosen by our PE master to play in school matches as he was guaranteed to bang them in the back of the net, along with a member of the opposing team.

I much preferred messing around, talking and chatting up girls. I found it easy to laugh and joke my way through my education. I thought that by being funny or playing the joker I'd gain favour with those around me. I would find pleasure in playing a joke on someone and not telling the rest of the world. I kept my cards close to my chest, just in case things went wrong. Only now can I let on that it was me who put one of our teacher's hats in the school fish tank, much to the amusement of the whole school. I was the one who threw eggs over the top of a wall at a teacher getting on a local bus. And it was me who put Deep Heat in the girls' trainers before PE. I was never thanked for it as I kept quiet, but I was even responsible for giving the whole school a day off when I tampered with the wiring which controlled the thermostat for the heating. With a small screwdriver I swapped a couple of wires round and to my amazement the following day the classrooms were too cold for us delicate young things to work in.

Occasionally if I was picked on by the other lads in my class, having a twin around came in handy, as Jeff was always there to sort the offenders out. Mind you, when he wasn't, I had to run like shit off a shovel, which is probably why in those days I was so skinny and also extremely fit.

I couldn't wait for the bell to ring at school as I had far more important things to do than study arithmetic and English. I would race out of class and chat to Mr Johnson, the school lollipop man. He was a mine of information and told me the most amazing stories whilst walking to and fro across Aintree Road. I learnt, among other things, that he was one of the few survivors of the *Titanic*. It was only when I saw him on a TV documentary that I realised the *Titanic* was a ship. I thought it was some hotel in Liverpool that had brought a coach party of pensioners down with food poisoning.

I didn't enjoy any sort of conformity. I joined the Boy Scouts for an hour, not even a chance to waggle me woggle. They told me that I was too rough during a game of five-a-side and asked me not to come back. I tried the St John Ambulance Brigade, not with the intention of saving lives but of saving a space at Liverpool's football ground for top matches. I got thrown out for standing on their one and only ping pong ball. They said I'd done it on purpose. After I threatened to knock out everyone in the group, to see how good they really were at First Aid, I was given my marching orders.

Eventually I found a niche that suited not only myself but Jeff, too. We joined the local church choir, not that we had any religious beliefs, but I heard that the money was good. You have to pay to be in the Scouts and the St John, but in the choir the uniforms were supplied free of charge and, not only did you not have to pay for the privilege of being a chorister, they paid you! The only stipulation was that you were available on Sundays. I became a rich man overnight. We used to get two shillings a wedding and two and six for funerals. It's a little sick looking back on it, but I was more than happy if a couple of people had copped it in a week. I didn't always let on to my folks that some weekends there had been three or more weddings. I'd say there had been just the one and fill myself up with sweets from the money I'd made from the rest. If I was questioned as to my whereabouts that day, I'd say I'd been out with Janice Allen.

Janice was my childhood sweetheart, a round, wholesome girl who most blokes in my year fancied. With the money I'd pocketed in the choir I'd buy her treats. I'd also nick daffodils from the local park and race with them to her house and escort her to school. This little bit of passionate thieving didn't last long. In Assembly one morning the local park keeper mounted the stage and, before he got to the microphone, I knew I was done for. He picked me out as the Great Daffodil Nicker of Derby Park. It was the only time I'd ever been caught for being naughty and I paid the price with detention, extra homework, cleaning duties and a good caning.

I have very few recollections of drink being around during my childhood, although my nan and grandad ran a pub at one time somewhere in Liverpool when Mum was a child. Occasionally our parents went out on their own for an evening, but if visitors came round they were only ever offered a cup of tea or at Christmas an old bottle of stout or a sherry from the back of the cupboard. Sometimes Mum and Dad would stop on the way home, after a long day out, for a half of lager and promise to bring us three screaming kids a bottle of pop each and a bag of crisps to polish off in the car.

I tried my first ever drink when I was ten. We went to a New Year's Eve party at a cousin's house. The adults – Mum and Dad included – had popped off to a local pub for an hour for some peace away from the kids. They'd left us lot behind to look after the trays of sandwiches, sausage rolls and crisps. There was also a small table filled with party drink. We promised not to touch a thing until their return. However, the temptation was too great for a group of hungry kids. We thought no one would really mind if we helped ourselves to a sausage roll and some refreshment. Whilst the others shared a bottle of lemonade, what I really fancied was a small bottle of Babycham. I'd seen a lot of adverts for it on television, but it never crossed my mind that it was an alcoholic beverage. I opened the bottle and what with being very thirsty from playing, I swigged back its contents.

After only a few minutes I started to feel dizzy and had problems trying to focus my eyes. I sat down and the whole room began to spin. Within minutes, I felt sick, heady and I was praying to God that it would soon stop. But it didn't. It was the worst experience of my life. I didn't realise that I was drinking alcohol.

Eventually, the adults returned to see the New Year in. I don't really remember too much after that as I went and laid down upstairs and fell asleep. The next thing I recall was trying to walk home with Mum and Dad. I think they knew I'd had something to drink and presumed I'd been slipped something by one of our relatives. Nothing was ever said about my antics and we went back to our house to break in our own New Year. I felt like a ton of sick and slept most of the following morning. From then on, every time I saw the advert for Babycham with a cute little Bambie cartoon deer flitting across the screen, it reminded me of what a night I'd had; a night, unlike the ad, that was not to be repeated.

I hated being drunk as I was a creative person and I liked to be in control of all my senses. I was very good with my hands and would spend hours in our garden shed with a hammer and chisel knocking out what I thought to be amazing arty wooden sculptures. Most of them ended up in the bin or Dad would use them to wedge up part of a ceiling.

I'd shown showbiz inclinations early on in my childhood. I'd save up my pocket and choir money for magic tricks and would regularly put on variety shows at home, usually ending up with my Des O'Connor impression. I always left the family audiences asking for more. I prided myself on the fact that no two shows were the same. I was a whiz with a hat and a cane and would practise for hours in the hope that one day I would be asked to step in for Des – and I reckoned I could at a moment's notice.

Jeff was quieter than me and had a talent for sport and art. He was a cracking footballer and played regularly for the school team, while Janice wanted to be an actress and spent all of her time at drama classes and rehearsing school plays.

Mum and Dad couldn't really afford to take us on expensive holidays abroad, so we used to go camping quite a bit and travel to such enticing climes as Wales and Cornwall. Dad was just like Crocodile Dundee and Mum was the Delia Smith of the camp fire – what she couldn't do with a tin of baked beans and a packet of sausages . . . It was a pity the weather wasn't always on our side. I remember one particular holiday in Scotland when Dad tried to put up a tent in a Force Ten gale on the banks of Loch Lomond. He looked like he was wrestling with a grizzly bear. He succeeded, but in the middle of the night the cross pole broke and after rescuing our bits and pieces we slept the rest of the night in the car, an Austin A40.

After many camping expeditions we tried a week on a canal barge travelling from Chester to Llangollen in north Wales. It was a life on the stagnant waves. A week relaxing on a long boat, basking on the foredeck, soaking up the sun and playing deck quoits with a carton of Kiora was not to be. During our conduit cruise, Janice tripped over Jeff's fishing net, went overboard and very nearly drowned. Dad dived in to rescue her and, after drying off, returned to the helm in his only other outfit, a suit, much to the amusement of other holidaymakers and the embarrassment of his children. The same night, when we decided to moor up, Dad leapt off the barge to tie it up. Unfortunately, Mum hadn't a clue what she was doing with the steering wheel and, drifting off into the reeds, the rope was lost. As Dad was venting his anger he stepped backwards and fell into the drink once again.

We never did reach Llangollen, because Dad tore a huge hole in the side of the boat whilst navigating one of the highest and narrowest of aqueducts. He, like me, has a fear of heights and nearly died of fright when he found himself so high up. His hands were shaking so much that he couldn't keep a straight line – hence the damage to our craft. Once we reached the other side we had to force him to do a quick U-turn and go back immediately, otherwise he wouldn't have plucked up the courage to do it again. We'd already done *Carry on Camping* and here we were making our own sequel, *Carry on Up the Canal*.

They were great holidays, but I was more than happy with the odd day out. It was on one of these days, in Rhyl, that I got my first taste of stardom. We went to a show on the seafront. It was music and lights all the way. There was a dashing compère who came on in various disguises, performing different routines. I thought I was the only one in the audience who could spot it was the same person each time. One minute he was a juggler, the next a clown and then he'd sing and dance with a top hat and cane, just like my mate Des O'Connor.

During the show they had a talent contest and asked for volunteers to come up on stage. This was it, the chance I'd been waiting for. All those years of coming out from behind our floral sofa and now I had the opportunity at last to walk out in front of some proper show curtains and perform in front of a real spotlight with an audience who hadn't seen the act. I remember racing down the aisle and Mum and Dad wondering what the hell their embarrassing son was up to. I felt a rush of adrenalin and loved every minute of it.

The compère asked me questions in front of the assembled masses. I gave him my name and age (nine) and said I would sing the only song I knew from beginning to end: a favourite little Des number of mine, 'I Pretend'. The pianist coped rather well: it should have run verse, chorus, verse, chorus, middle eight and end, but I think I went middle eight, end, chorus, verse. Nevertheless, I gave it my best shot. I looked cute in those days and to my surprise I was pronounced the winner. I couldn't believe it and nor could my family. I'd beaten the rest of those top class entertainers! Close second was a kid doing an impression of a muscle man – he looked more like he had a stomach full of worms; third was a twelve-year-old tap dancer from Torquay in a glittery leotard. It wasn't much competition, but at least I'd won, singing my trusty Des number. My gateway to the world of showbusiness was now open.

Not long after my winning performance I was approached by a talent scout called Mr Jackson. He was keen on my joining a concert party called The Happy Wanderers that toured the Northern club circuit. I don't think Mum and Dad were too struck on the idea, but I, having tasted success, was more than ready to sign up.

I worked religiously on my act at home. I decided not to do magic – I thought the cup and ball trick wasn't exactly a wow with the audience and I didn't fancy being booed off at my very first gig. I settled on being a song and dance man and, after relentless nagging, my Mum and Dad let me join The Happy Wanderers Concert Party.

My life became one big tour of working men's clubs in such exciting places as Chorley, Eccleston and downtown Preston. I sang my Des ditties and added a few Al Jolson numbers to make people think I had more of an act. It was a tough life on the road to fame and fortune.

Sometimes we would go to hospitals, hospices and old folks' homes. These audiences would have clapped anyone as they were grateful for any kind of entertainment, especially when it was free. I would go on stage and do my three numbers. I always had a fourth standing by just in case I was asked to do an encore. I hasten to add, though, that I invariably sang my fourth song, whether the audience wanted it or not. A cough was enough for me. And if someone got up to go to the loo I took it as a standing ovation.

By this time, Janice, Jeff and I were also working as a trio with the fantastically original name of The Chegwins – a kind of mini Osmonds – earning anything from ten bob to a pound. During our time together we won the odd award and cup as well, and were regularly seen in the local paper, which gave me quite a buzz when it was mentioned to me by mates at school.

Time passed and I auditioned for a TV show called *Junior Show Time*, produced by Jess Yates, father of Paula Yates. A children's variety show made by Yorkshire Television, it basically had every spoilt, precocious brat in the country appearing on it! My first television performance was quite a nerve-racking experience. My biggest setback was that I wasn't allowed to sing my show-stopping Des ditty. The production team much preferred the Louis Armstrong number 'What a Wonderful World' that I sang as second choice at the audition. The recording was at the City Varieties Theatre in Leeds. Also appearing on the show was the film star Jack Wilde, who had played the Artful Dodger in the film *Oliver*. He was a huge star at the time, and I remember looking at him signing autographs and wondering whether one day people would be asking for mine. Also there was his agent and manager, June Collins, mother of Phil Collins. Luckily, my performance couldn't have been all that bad as my parents were approached after the show by June Collins who thought I could make a go of it in the entertainment world. But, if I was to succeed, London was the place to try and stage school, rather than a comprehensive, was the place to be.

It was a difficult time for the whole family. On the one hand I wanted to take that next step, but at the same time I didn't want to leave home and live in London. June Collins was on the phone to us shortly after my first telly to ask if not only myself but also Jeff would come down to the Smoke and audition for a new Children's Film Foundation film called *Egghead's Robot*. They were looking for identical twins, one to play the part of Egghead, a boffinlike kid, the other to play the robot he builds in his own likeness to do all the things he can't do, like play cricket and run fast. After a bit of hesitation we went down to London and, to our surprise, we were offered the job. Jeff and I were to become film stars. I was to play the Egghead and Jeff, although a little uncertain at first, was happy to take on the role of the robot. It had a star-studded cast headed by Roy Kinnear, Richard Wattis and Patricia Routledge (Mrs Bucket). Our only disappointment was having to stay away from home for the six weeks of filming.

We stayed with a family close to the stage school in west London. I remember days when I couldn't wait to get into make-up and wardrobe and start filming and also days when I was crying in my bed at night because I was homesick. We saw Mum and Dad every weekend and they always told us that if we ever wanted to come home, regardless of film contracts and letting people down, we could do so at a moment's notice.

After I'd finished making the film I made the decision to stay on in London and continue my theatrical and academic career at the Barbara Speake Stage School. Thankfully, Jeff did likewise. I think he, like me, enjoyed his acting debut and quite fancied doing some more. I was particularly grateful for him staying on as he would be there to look after me.

At first, I hated the place. It wasn't the sort of school that Jeff and I were used to. The boys didn't get changed into footie gear for a good kicking and an hour's worth of headbutting on the pitch. Instead, we were sent off to the cloakroom to change into a pair of tights for sixty minutes of ballet. Gone were the days of good old biology lessons and arithmetic. We had to suffer vocal training and heavy sessions of ballet theory, jazz dancing and tap dancing lessons. If the boys in Bootle could have seen us prancing round in tights, we'd have been hoisted up high and had our balls chopped off.

I see now, in retrospect, that the things I thought were silly at the time helped develop my confidence. And, to this day, I've found that the things I was taught, like how to do a pirouette, cartwheel, tap dance, improvise, read aloud, play the guitar and piano and project my voice, have certainly come in handy with various jobs I've been asked to do.

Shortly after my film debut, I auditioned for the stage show *Mame*, starring Ginger Rogers. I got the job, but unfortunately after three weeks of rehearsals I had to give it up because the hours were so variable. The London Education Authority, quite rightly, would not allow any youngster under the age of fourteen to work for so long in a stage show without attending school. However, all was not lost. I may not have been allowed to do a long-running stage show but I could still carry on performing in films and television, as long as the hours were regulated and I had an educational tutor and a chaperon with me at all times.

I felt I was one of the lucky ones at stage school. I was there because I wanted a career in showbusiness. Some of the kids seemed to be there because their parents wanted to relive their own childhoods. I'd seen parents picking their little darlings up from school in BMWs and Mercedes and bragging to friends about which commercial their spoilt brat had appeared in recently. I suppose having a child in a private school, and a stage school at that, was a good one to mention at dinner parties.

I had to work very hard when I was there. My school fees were paid out of what I earned from the jobs I did, so I had to work hard and pass most of the auditions I went for if I wanted to stay at the school. Being put into this position, I felt I had to do a lot of lying and cheating. If I was auditioning for a television commercial, I'd tell the producer and director that this was the first commercial I'd been offered. Little did they know that I had already made quite a few. I was the boy in the Robinson's Lemon Barleywater commercial. I advertised Pepsi (before Michael Jackson), Tizer soft drinks, and even modelled underpants in the Freemans catalogue. Nine times out of ten I'd get the job I was going for. My technique was to make sure that after each audition I left the client with something to remember me by.

I'd make up stories. My favourite was that I'd just met Michael Caine on the London Underground and I didn't have a pen to get his autograph. I'd spoken to him in between tube stops and while doing so I'd spilt a can of drink over his trousers. My thinking was that, after they'd seen forty or more kids like myself for the same job, with a story like that they were more likely to remember me than the others. Believe it or not, it seemed to work.

Every audition was a challenge. I went to one where they were looking for a kid to play the part of a 52-year-old midget who could do acrobatics. I sneaked off to the loo to practise my headstands and cartwheels. As my legs were straddled either side of the hand dryer, a gentleman came in. It turned out he was the producer. He gave me the job, not because of my ability, but for my enthusiasm to get the job.

I never stopped working. I flitted from TV set to film location. I worked with them all: Peter Sellers, Ronnie Barker, David Jason, Brian Glover, Tom Courtenay, Michael Hordern, Martin Shaw, Francesca Annis, Nerys Hughes, Alison Steadman, Clive Dunn and more. I was a child star and my stageshow buddies included Simon Le Bon, Christopher Guard and Russell Grant. One of the London papers ran a story about me and my work with the headline 'The Gob Stopper Millionaire'.

Jeff and I lived in digs less than half a mile away from the school with four other boys. Our chaperon/landlady, Mrs Roache, was a single parent with a daughter called Lesley. Mrs Roache also worked at the school as a dinner lady. Most days, what we had for lunch at school was brought home for dinner in the evening.

I don't know why she opened her house to the kids at the school. The money she was paid to look after us couldn't have been very much and she never seemed to be that keen on having us around. We stayed there for about eight months. I was pleased to leave, and Jeff and I eventually moved to St John's Wood, home of the stars.

Life was made a lot happier with the Angel family and Mrs Angel was certainly some angel. She seemed to spend all her money on the kids that lived with her. I remember one time she'd won a few quid on the pools and took us all to a camping shop to buy tents and sleeping bags so she could take us away for weekends. As long as we kept her house tidy, she was like putty in our hands. We built tree houses and played football till the lawn was worn through. The neighbours thought we lowered the tone of the area. Their driveways were filled with Jags and Rollers; ours was filled with a tatty old Bedford van.

Next door there lived a doctor whose evening barbecues were often spoilt by us kids hanging over his twelve-foot garden wall asking for a chicken leg. One time when he had friends over he turned down our request, so he and his party mates had to suffer the consequences – a drenching from the hose pipe. When he came round to complain, Mrs Angel used the old one: 'Boys will be boys'.

Our other neighbour was Bob Monkhouse. We didn't see much of Bob, but we did spend a lot of time in his garden. In between the odd game of football, we'd nick apples off his trees. One day when we thought he was away we ventured into his property and to our surprise he was there and in no uncertain terms told us where to go.

When Jeff and I turned sixteen, we decided that we'd had enough of living with other people. We spoke to Mum and Dad and they too agreed that as we were both earning, we'd be far happier in a place of our own. I was doing the odd acting job and Jeff had now given up his acting career and started full-time work in the record industry.

Our first rented flat was a mile away from the BBC in Shepherd's Bush. It was owned by a German chap who kept two spider monkeys on the premises. Some days he let them loose in the landings and hall areas. They were vicious buggers. I used to prepare myself to run up to my flat like Indiana Jones in the Temple of Doom being chased by that stone ball. I'd turn the key quietly in the lock in case they were on the rampage, take a deep breath and do a Roger Bannister up the first flight of stairs. Nine times out of ten they'd hear me come in and start screeching. The clambering noises would reverberate round the hallway and I had only seconds to get the key into the lock and gain the safety of my flat. One day, my timing was to pot and one of the monkeys managed to leap on to my back. I'm sure its intentions were friendly, but I was in no mood for hugging. I swivelled round quickly and managed to shake the thing loose. It hit the opposite wall like a student rucksack as its mate looked on in startled silence. From then on, every time I went in or out of the place I carried an umbrella. I remember the landlord asking me why I was carrying a brolly when it was eighty degrees outside and not a chance of rain. I made an excuse that because I was fair skinned I used it as a sunshade. I couldn't tell him it was to knock seven bells of shit out of his monkeys.

I never drank much in my youth. Occasionally if I was invited to a party I would have the odd glass of Strongbow cider. I drank it because it was cheap and it was usually available to under eighteens in the supermarket. I also found that because of the age group at parties it was normally in abundance. I never, ever got drunk. I remember my dad once advising me to line my stomach with something. He recommended a pint of milk or at least some food before going out for the night. I lived in fear of what would happen the first time I consumed a proper drink, so I always downed a pint of milk before any festive function. On one occasion, on the way to a mate's house, I spilt about half a pint down my party outfit. It wasn't until I was doing a bit of bopping that I started to perspire. The smell was enough to make the other disco boppers leave the floor. Even I had to wince at the smell of sweat and half a pint of curdling Gold Top.

Jeff and I stuck together through thick and thin. We eventually ended up living in West Ealing, a suburb of London. I was finding it difficult to get work. There weren't many parts for spotty juveniles, so I had to make do with the odd bit of television extra work. For about twelve quid a day I made up the numbers in a football team and ran with the crowds in the odd television commercial. It didn't do my ego much good. Gone were the days when I was the star of the film. I played young Robin in *Robin Hood Junior*, Fleance in Roman Polanski's *Macbeth*, a cameo role in *Black Beauty, The Liver Birds, Z Cars*, commercial after commercial and three West End stage shows, including nine months of singing and dancing in *The Good Old Bad Old Days* with Anthony Newley.

At this point I decided to have another go at making a singing career for myself and joined a band called Kenny. They made it to Number Four in the charts with a song called 'The Bump', but I left because of a dispute with the management about money. The rest of the lads were content with fame, but not fortune. I wanted both, so I left. Next I got a part in a new television comedy series on the ITV network called *The Wackers*, all about a Liverpudlian family and very similar to the series *Bread*. Sadly, it didn't last too long. There were so many complaints about its bad language that Mary Whitehouse succeeded in having it taken off.

At the age of eighteen I became bored and was looking for something a bit different. I was watching Frank Bough on television one night when I had the idea that I'd like to be a television presenter. I was no newsreader, so I wrote to the head of children's programmes at the BBC with an idea for a children's chat show with me as the host. As a result of the letter they called me in for an audition, which I passed. The next thing I knew, I was asked to be one of the presenters on a new 'live' Saturday morning show called *Swap Shop*, with Noel Edmonds.

I remember my very first meeting with Mr Blobby's mate. I had to film some trailers for the start of the series at a lido in Middlesex. I got there early and saw Mr Edmonds arrive in a dashing Range Rover. As I was about to be the co-presenter of the series, I thought it best to introduce myself, so wandered over to his motor. We had a very brief chat after which Noel asked if I had a pen and paper so that he could give me his autograph. I was utterly gob smacked. Welcome to the world of television presentation. This is how the other half live. Superstars trading autographs with each other. I'd got his signature but he wasn't too keen on asking for mine.

The first *Swap Shop* was on 8 October 1976 and its success was phenomenal. It would have blown anyone away. Viewing figures went sky high and I became nationally known as 'Cheggers'. It was instant recognition from the off. Wherever I went, people would ask for my autograph. I was in great demand. I opened shop after shop and even had to employ a bouncer to be with me nearly twenty-four hours a day to look after my welfare. For some unknown reason people seemed to have this urge wherever I went to beat me up.

Through the programme's success they gave me my own series called *Cheggers Plays Pop*. It was recorded in Manchester and had all sorts of hip bands appearing on it, such as The Undertones, Bow Wow Wow and Altered Images. It was voted one of the top music shows in the *New Musical Express*. One year I was on the telly in the morning with *Swap Shop* and then I'd pop up on the screen later in the day with a game show called *Anything Goes*.

If you missed me on the telly you could always tune into Radio One where I co-presented the weekend morning shows live with Tony Blackburn. It came to a point where you couldn't turn on the box, switch on your radio or pick up a magazine without seeing me. I was reported to be one of the top children's presenters in the country! I knew I'd made it when I couldn't walk down the street without people shouting 'Wanker!'

They must have thought I was earning a fortune. Little did they know that in those days I was receiving £45 a week for my time on *Swap Shop* and, to be honest, although I had the success, there never seemed to be much money around.

I contemplated buying a small flat on my own but due to lack of resources went halves on a mews house in Twickenham with Maggie Philbin, one of the co-presenters of the Saturday morning programme. I never seemed to spend that much time in the place. I was either out doing personal appearances or at late night discos. But I was happy to be investing my money rather than throwing it away in some London bedsit.

Saturday morning television took up a lot of my time. On the outside broadcasts I had many a heavy drinking session the evening before a show. I never got totally blotto, but I did enjoy a night out with the lads. I was working with a producer at the time who, in true BBC children's fashion, was keen to make sure his little starlet went to bed early so that I was bright-eyed and bushy-tailed for the morning. He was a little overpowering at times and I remember on one occasion he went through my entire suitcase to make sure I'd brought with me a multi-coloured pullover and some bright jeans to wear on the programme in the morning. Little did our caring producer know that after I went to my room at nine o'clock, the rest of the outside broadcast team would call me once he'd retired and we'd sneak out of the hotel for a night on the town. Some nights I'd stayed up so late with the crew it didn't seem worth going to bed. I only had enough time for a shower and a shave, then out with the team to present a live show.

I remember one night ending up in a rough pub in Wigan. The place was full of blokes. I thought we'd got it wrong and ended up in some gay club. Not that I have anything against gay people, but my idea of a good night out was chatting up the ladies. Myself and the rest of the team found what seemed to be the only lady in the place and I chatted to her for quite some time. She was very pretty and extremely friendly. She exuded confidence. I didn't have to wait long to find out why. She asked me to hold on to her drink, explaining she wouldn't be long. I thought it was my lucky night as she slipped out of her skintight dress, which she dropped to the floor. I was only eighteen and there right in front of me was a lady who I'd only known for five minutes with hardly anything on. It was more like 'Cheggers Plays Cock' as she left the bar and headed for the dance floor. I'd been chatting to the evening's entertainment. The place was full of fellas waiting for the stripper to come on. She was very good!

I had lots of great times during this period, but I never really got drunk. I'd always manage not to have that one too many. In the back of my mind I knew that when I was working I had a job to do and I was too proud to let drink affect my work. Even socially, I held myself back from that extra tipple.

Brother Jeff was on a roll, too. He seemed to be working all hours in the record industry. He'd got himself a job working for Jonathan King promoting records. However, as time went by, we started to see less and less of each other, as each of us created our own circle of new friends.

There was a lot of press speculation that something was going on between myself and Maggie Philbin. She had joined the *Swap Shop* team on the second series and we had got on really well from the off. We did a lot of filming together and eventually ended up presenting most of the live outside broadcasts together. We were the younger members of the team and we shared similar interests. We'd go to the cinema together and eat out most of the time together. Eventually, we even asked our BBC producers to book adjoining hotel rooms so that we could go through programme notes the night before a show, if necessary.

No one knew that we had started dating and we were happy to keep it that way, because of our fear of any publicity affecting our work. The *Sun* newspaper had found out that we were sharing a house and ran a story claiming they'd been to the house and were sure nothing was going on, that our relationship was purely platonic.

No one knew the real truth, not even our friends in television. That we were in love. We kept it secret for a long time but eventually, in early 1982, Maggie asked me to marry her. Our wedding was announced to the press and we were married on 4 September of that year.

It was a fairy-tale romance and it appeared that most of the nation was eager to express their approval. Cards and letters came from all over the country, and abroad, to wish us well. I was as happy as Larry and spent a long time racing up and down the country so as I could be home most nights with Maggie.

The next two years were wonderful. We found that jointly we could afford a bit of the high life. Eventually we decided that it was time to move out of our semi in Twickenham and find something with a little more room.

CHAPTER THREE

In 1984 Maggie and I moved to a house on the borders of Hampshire and Berkshire. I wasn't too keen to move out of London. I was far too young. I was born a townie and I didn't relish the idea of life in the country. As far as I was concerned, the Sticks were where you went on holiday. As a kid, I had enjoyed our family outings to the country but I was always glad to get back to the city. Smog, car fumes, shops, public toilets – *Bliss!* It took nearly two years to find a 'suitable' house.

Eventually, we bought a seventeenth-century farmhouse with seven acres of land. I couldn't afford it and it needed piles of work doing to it. The estate agent's pictures were very flattering. There were lots of rooms: four bedrooms and a bathroom upstairs; downstairs had a big kitchen, breakfast room, hallway, dining room and sitting room. There was also an annexe with a kitchen, living room, bedroom and bathroom. Outside there was a large barn, two stables, a tack room and potting shed, plus two paddocks, a kitchen garden and an old tumbled-down forge.

We bought the place from an old lady of ninety-six and still going strong. She appeared to be keen to get shot of the place quickly. She wanted to live out the rest of her life with her grandson somewhere on the east coast. We went back several times to view the house and on each occasion I enjoyed chatting to her about the days when she played a nifty game of golf and how she now invited her friends round for an afternoon of bridge. She was definitely from the old school. The house's contents didn't really suit it, though. It was full of huge ornate vases, paintings, large antique furniture, curios and knick-knacks that were obviously once set in a house of equal grandeur and stature.

Once, before leaving, the old lady asked whether we would keep the young girl on. Apparently, she had had a local lady working for her for some time, who would be out of a job after she'd gone. By chance, we were looking for someone to help with a bit of washing and ironing, so it suited us to have someone who knew the house and was just down the road. Someone who could keep an eye on the place if we were away for a while. The young girl she spoke of happened to arrive as we were about to leave. By the look of her she'd been collecting bus tokens for a long while and I wondered whether to ask her if she had by any chance received her telegram from the Queen yet. She told me that she was seventy-six years old and was a whiz with a duster. When I enquired how much she charged, she said five pounds. I was taken aback somewhat, as the very, very young girl we already had cleaning for us was only three pounds an hour. Maybe she looked after the garden and did a bit of building work as well for such an exorbitant wage. I put in an offer of three pounds fifty, which was immediately turned down. In her warm Hampshire accent she said, 'I couldn't possibly work for that.' I was all ready to find someone else when it transpired that she had worked at the house for more than forty years and five pounds was her total wage for the week! For that she'd cooked, washed, ironed and cleaned and she was flabbergasted when I told her that we were willing to pay her more than that per day for all her hard work.

At first I was quite happy to play lord of the manor. I'd bought all the country gear: a Barbour jacket, a cap and the obligatory green wellies. I had even bought a dog to complete the look.

I bragged to my London mates about living the 'good life' and how healthy I was. Of course, I never let on about the bad bits. The bats, the bugs, the rats and nasties. At one time, I thought about getting a sponsorship deal with Nippon fly spray, I used so much of the stuff getting rid of the army of creepy crawlies that invaded my house as soon as it became dark. And talking of the dark, I hated it. I was used to a bit of neon street lighting coming through my windows. I was so frightened that I would make sure everything was done during daylight hours so that I didn't have to venture out after the sun had gone down. One night, I was forced to go out and grab a bucket of coal for the fire. I was deeply embarrassed when a neighbour walked up the driveway to discover me with a tennis racket held above my head to fend off the bats that used to dive bomb me and which I thought might get caught in my hair.

For a short while, life in the country was OK, but as time ticked by the novelty was wearing thin. I wasn't into the horsy set – horses were for people that looked like them. I missed the

Seven Eleven. There were no clubs and the locals' idea of a late night was being in the pub for last orders. Most of the pubs in the area had pushed the real country folk out and now they were filled with the Hooray Henrys. They'd monopolise the pool table, talk loudly, and in between mouthfuls of whisky and soda answer their portable phones. I preferred mixing with the genuine country people. Life during the week was much more enjoyable as then most of the weekenders had returned to the city to brag about their two days of shooting pheasant and the odd farmer in rural England.

By this time, I'd been given a horse as a Christmas present, which had to be ridden once a day, every day. It also had to be fed, mucked out and turned out. A lie-in was a rarity, as I had to be there to cater for its creature comforts first thing in the morning. At first, I loved that horse and went to great lengths to learn about its anatomy, its past history, and even bought books on equine management. I wasn't too unhappy to find out that my horse had previously been a racehorse; in fact I searched high and low to find some record of its past wins. I was ecstatic when I found out it had come fourth in a race at Chepstow. Sad thing was, there were only three others in the race!

She was called Ding Dong, as her previous owner reckoned she ran like a ding dong bell! He wasn't wrong. The bloody animal never stopped running. It was like a generator that was on the go twenty-four hours a day. When out riding, I was sitting on Mount Etna – any excuse and the thing would erupt. I became a bit of a joke locally as me and my kangaroo hopped up the village. I could just imagine what the locals thought: Here comes Cheggers and his celebrity horse. Something had to change, and my immediate thoughts turned to employing a local person who would relish the opportunity of riding a horse free of charge.

We eventually found a young girl called Maria. At the time she was already working with horses in a livery yard in the village, where we'd kept our horses until we'd had some building work done to accommodate them at home. I'd already met her employer, a real horsy type: large, loud and lacking tact. When she told me once that she'd broken nearly every bone in her body I wondered whether her clients at the yard had done the damage or whether she'd really fallen off that many times. I went out riding with her once. During our trek, she saw a rabbit. Without thinking, she slid off her horse and clumped it several times over the head with a thick piece of wood. I was devastated, I couldn't believe what she'd just done. I was aware that farmers shot the odd rabbit, but a bit of bunny bashing was not on. She later told me that the rabbit had myxomatosis and it was better to put it out of its misery quickly than let it suffer. She had restored my faith in country ways and, secretly, I quite liked her after that.

When Maggie and I asked Maria to come and join us, she leapt at the chance, as she was earning a pittance. She relished the idea of earning some more money whilst I relished the thought of sleeping in and also of watching someone else ride my bucking bronco.

Maria eventually moved into one of the back bedrooms and started to live with us on a permanent basis. It was useful to have someone at the house twenty-four hours a day as both Maggie and I spent a lot of time away working. Maria became head cook and bottle washer of Lime Tree Cottage and no job was too small. She even doubled as a secretary-cum-PA to both Maggie and I and, if pushed, as well as mucking out the horses she would act as a heavy on some of my late evening disco shows.

During this time I was like Michael Jackson. I had collected a menagerie of three dogs, five cats, two ducks, three horses and a pig, plus a housekeeper, a groom, a builder/handyman, two gardeners and a driver. Three cars stood in the driveway, along with a horse trailer and a bike in case of emergencies. The deep freeze was stocked with the best Marks and Spencer had to offer and I bought a wine rack which I filled with my favourite red and white wines.

I drank most days, usually at least a bottle of wine, if not more, depending on my mood. I loved a drink at the end of a hard day's work. I couldn't wait to get home and open a bottle of wine. As time went by I'd wind down at the end of the day with a can of lager, followed by a bottle of wine, then I'd polish off a brandy before retiring to bed. Some nights I'd stagger a little up the stairs and, during this period of what I would call my novice years, I would even tell Maria and Maggie that I thought I'd overdone it. It was a laugh and I would enjoy the feeling of going to bed slightly heady.

My daughter Rose was born on 29 April 1988. Maggie had gone through a lot of trouble to bring her into the world and I enjoyed being left holding the baby while she recovered. I now felt like a responsible adult. I was a dab hand at changing nappies, bathing and bringing up wind. I was grateful for feeding times, as Maggie breastfed and it gave me the chance to catch up on some sleep.

Shortly after Rose was born I acquired a taste for whisky. I never bothered with the old malts and Scotches that had taken forty years of blending and maturing, just the odd bottle of Bells that I would buy at the off licence on the way home. I used to mix it with some coke or water and have a glass or two with my evening meal, in place of a bottle of wine. It was a drink I felt comfortable with, something I felt that really suited me. A glass of whisky, a small cigar and a Chinese takeaway was my idea of heaven.

To everyone outside, life was supposedly wonderful, but I had to work very hard to keep it. It meant travelling the length and breadth of Great Britain, from shop openings in the Shetlands to garden fêtes in Folkstone. I'd always be back late and then continue to write 200 tunes in my recording studio for television. At one time, I was directing videos, writing scripts and recording a new series for the Beeb. I had to do it to pay for a lifestyle I wasn't really keen on any more.

As a result of chasing bills, I was permanently shattered, my diet was terrible and I'd forgotten what it was like to put my feet up and read the *Beano*.

I had also got involved in a considerable amount of charity work. I was devastated when I saw pictures on television and in the newspapers of the appalling atrocities in Romania and I felt I had to do something to help. I got in touch with the relief fund for Romania and offered my services. I was grateful when they contacted me later to ask if I was free to go and help distribute medical supplies, clothing and food in some of the poorer areas of Romania that had yet to be serviced by any charity. Later the same week I found myself at Heathrow airport, packed and ready to go. I was keen to do anything to help, but I also wondered whether I would be able to get a drink out there.

For the first time in my life, drink became a priority. I felt that I couldn't leave the country without something to take with me. I felt that a glass of whisky would help me to relax. When I didn't have something to drink, I found it difficult to go to sleep and some nights I would get out of bed and head downstairs for a cigarette and a warm glass of Bells.

The night before my departure, I went to the off licence and purchased twenty half bottles of whisky to consume during my visit. It was madness, but I had to do it, just in case I couldn't get anything over there. I even thought of an excuse if anyone ever discovered them in my suitcase. I'd say I was taking them out to use as bribes. On reaching the airport, I discovered that the rest of my party of dogooders included a reporter and a photographer from the *News of the World*. I truly feared that someone would check the contents of my bags, but luckily no one did.

My time was well spent in Romania. A party of trucks had set off from London the week before our arrival but we had a few days to sort out where best to distribute their much-needed contents before they arrived. The news footage and the pictures I'd seen prior to my visit in no way made it clear enough to people at home how appalling the situation really was.

When I visited hospitals, hospices and homes, I couldn't believe what I saw: kids lying in rusty makeshift beds, row after row of them, lying in shit and covered in open sores. The stench and the flies were unbelievable. Even the toughest of lorry drivers cried as we distributed clothes and some food to the needy and the medical supplies to the so-called hospitals, which were no more than run-down buildings with sick people in them and a few doctors to wash down the odd patient. The two chaps from the newspaper forgot their impending deadline and mucked in with helping as much as was physically possible during our visit. I drank while I was there and even declined an invitation for a booze-up with the lorry drivers one night; the news reporter commented on my restraint. Little did he know that I had my own supply and drank alone in my room till I fell asleep.

At one time my home seemed to be operating as a bed and breakfast facility for the people I had working for me. It wasn't unusual for my driver to stay overnight, or the odd musician who had come to record some backing tracks to kip down for the night. Visitors were very rarely turned away. One time, a vet came up the drive to examine one of our feline boarders who wasn't too well. She examined the kitten and returned the following day to check on its progress. The vet staggered up our driveway and stumbled into the house. It was obvious by her antics that something was very wrong. We weren't immediately sure what the problem was, but she was in no fit state to return to her work nor in fact her home. Maggie suggested that she move in with us for a while until she felt better. It later transpired that she was very ill with some form of M.E. She set up home in one of the back bedrooms. A month later, she moved out. Not out of the house, but into one of our bigger double bedrooms. She said the bed in the back room was too hard and she found it more comfortable in mine. The bed might have been a little hard, but one day our groom committed a major sin: she was told by the vet that her morning bowl of Frosties were too soft. Six months later and with no contribution to her own upkeep, she eventually left. She gave us a painting of some cats so we could remember her visit. Kind though it was, the picture of her leaving was enough for me.

It had been mentioned on many occasions, by my mates, that I drank more than most people, but I took no notice. In retrospect, I found that I was never, ever content with just a couple of glasses of anything; I would always empty the bottle, even if I was the only person drinking from it. I really enjoyed my drink and even started to encourage the odd glass of sherry during a planning meeting at the BBC when going over a script for a show. After a meeting I'd suggest heading up to the BBC bar before I headed off to catch my train home.

Although I drank most days, for some unknown reason I never suffered from a hangover. Sometimes, but very rarely, I'd wake up feeling a little groggy, but one cup of coffee and two fags later I'd be as bright as a button and ready to take on the day. I could quite happily ease off the sauce for a few days or more, depending on what I was working on.

Mind you, any longer than that and the yearning for a relaxing drink would return. At that time, I'd justified my drinking to myself by making comparisons with some of my best mates or colleagues. 'I don't drink as much as Harry', 'I never drink before lunch time', 'I can hold my own'.

Occasionally, just to convince myself that I didn't have a problem with the amber nectar, I'd stop for a short while. I'd even brag to people at work that I was going on the wagon for a bit. No half measures for me. If I was to go to such lengths, then the whole world had to know. Two days without a drink and all around me were made aware that I'd completed this valiant task and come through with flying colours. Then I'd gasp a sigh of relief and plunge into the nearest off licence to buy my first bottle of whisky in what seemed ages. I'd keep the survival story alive for the next few weeks, suggesting to my mates and colleagues that they try it some time. Might do 'em some good to go on the wagon for a while. Lose some weight! Get healthy!

It never, ever crossed my mind to think that one day I might have a problem controlling my drinking habits. That one day I'd be reduced to sifting through the empties for that last drop in the bottle or that I'd even resort to hiding my booze for fear of discovery. That I would manipulate close friends into buying drink for me; that I would hire and fire the people who drove me around the country, depending on whether they became too suspicious of my drinking habits. That I'd persuade my doctor to give me pills to help wean me off the drink, then abuse the drugs I'd been given. That I'd have this uncontrolled obsession with drink taking up every minute of my day. I'd lie and cheat to get it. If I didn't have enough money, I'd run up tabs at local shops, get courier companies to fetch it for me and borrow money from my best mates. It never crossed my mind that I would drink anything I could lay my hands on – Night Nurse, mouthwash and more. In the early days, I wasn't all out to get pissed. My drinking was more than twenty-one or two units a week, in fact it was probably twenty-one a night, but it wasn't a problem. I never hit anyone, or embarrassed myself or my friends by my behaviour. Like everyone else, I enjoyed a drink, but deep down I was curious to find out why I'd wake up feeling like I'd slept the night in a tumble dryer.

Unbeknown to me, alcohol, like a piece of ivy, was weaving its way into my body. I was beginning to become chemically dependent on booze.

Oddly enough, I remember the day I started drinking in the mornings. I was working away from home and had ended up in Peterborough. I had been on the road for more than five days with my two-hour stage show touring the country. I'd had it, I was all out, totally exhausted. My best mate at the time and I had just done yet another personal appearance and we had ended up staying overnight in a hotel. It was the perfect hotel, the kind of place I love. It had a cheap and cheerful menu serving traditional English food and a huge bar open to the public, a pool table and a couple of slot machines. Who could ask for more? I had a great time. We took on the locals at pool, darts and drinking. I thought I'd done rather well until I was told in the morning that I'd blacked out during one of the drinking challenges and had had to be carried off to my hotel bedroom.

I'd never heard of a blackout before. It's when you literally drink yourself into oblivion and collapse. When I woke up in the morning, totally unaware of my antics the night before, I had trouble getting out of bed and I felt sick and dizzy. Before meeting up with my working colleague I'd already made friends with the hotel toilet and was considering staying for another night. I was in no fit state to leave. My mate told me that he'd noticed some decline in my behaviour as the evening progressed. I had been telling dirty jokes – unusual for me at the time, as I was very image conscious. I had also taken my top off for a bit of arm wrestling. Unheard of. Eventually, I had collapsed in a heap and had had to be escorted off to my bed. Very unusual. All of which I didn't remember.

I was feeling pretty rough and was in no mood to carry on working that day, but I had to. I'd heard of various cures and contemplated having what they call 'the hair of the dog'. I was told it sometimes helps to have a drink when you are feeling rough as it eases you out of your groggy stupor. Before I checked out I opened the mini bar in my room and, without thinking, helped myself to a couple of miniature whiskies. After a short while I started to feel better. I was aware that I'd just topped myself up, but it certainly helped. I stopped wanting to be sick; I was able to get my act together, although I still felt a little tipsy. This was far better than acting like a grumpy old man with a seven-inch nail stuck in his head. For the rest of that day, I continued to drink – not a lot, but just enough to keep me topped up and able to work.

Without realising the consequences of that morning's actions, I was well and truly hooked. I didn't drink every morning, only when I felt the need to clear my head. But once I started to drink I would carry on throughout the entire day.

I was like a hamster on a treadmill and some days I couldn't get off. There seemed to be no reasonable excuse for having a drink – I wasn't depressed, lonely or angry – I just seemed to enjoy the effect it had on me. I felt it gave me a bit of confidence, the edge on other people. I was happy to relax in the garden soaking up the sun with a huge glass of whisky. If I was invited round to a friend's for lunch, I would bring my own bottle of Scotch to save downing most of theirs.

People were becoming aware of my excessive drinking. One night I argued with Maggie about how much I'd drunk that day. I knowingly challenged all claims as to what I'd consumed.

I eventually lost the battle when the bin outside was emptied and I had to admit to polishing off a whole bottle of whisky and six cans of lager. Even then, I had some supplies which hadn't been discovered, ready to consume during the evening. I admitted defeat and promised to cut down.

I tried a couple of days without a drink but I was finding it hard. I got angry with people, I couldn't sleep and for the first time ever I started to shake and sweat. Little did I know that I was going through withdrawal symptoms. I found myself in a quandary, a bit of a hole. I was working from home at the time, so I wasn't able to have a drink without some kind of rumpus. I thought about popping down to the pub for lunch – at least there I could have a quiet pint or two. Eventually I went out to the local shop and bought a bottle of whisky and six cans of lager.

That evening I produced one of the cans to have with my dinner. There were no complaints from Maggie or Maria to me having just one can, but what they didn't realise was that every so often I'd pop out of the living room to the kitchen, which was quite a walk and well out of earshot, and bring in another. It was assumed that I'd held on to the one can I'd started the evening with, when in fact I'd managed to consume all six plus at least half of my bottle in the cupboard.

Every day I replenished my supply for the evening and carried on with my antics for a long while with no one any the wiser. Sometimes, when the house was empty, I'd have free rein and was able to drink from morning till night. I'd usually fall asleep on the sofa or struggle up to a back bedroom and collapse. Then I started to wet the bed, but I blamed the dog or said that I had spilled the glass of water I kept by the bed during the night. I was found pissing out of a bedroom window, relieving myself in a walk-in wardrobe and out cold on the kitchen floor. All of which I blamed on my heavy workload.

I wasn't really doing much work at the time, though, and I took comfort in a drink. I liked the feeling it gave me. I felt that once I'd had a drink I was back on form. Until now, I had never used it to drown my sorrows, or as a crutch to help me get through a difficult period of my life. But this was about to change.

By now, I hadn't worked on children's television for a few years. As I was told by Anna Hulme, the newly appointed head of BBC children's programmes, I was too old to present their shows.

I remember being taken out to lunch on 12 January 1987 for the first time in over eleven years of working for the Beeb. I had the feeling that I wasn't being treated to any kind of thank-you lunch. We met at a very posh London restaurant. White tablecloths, crystal glasses and a French menu with no subtitles. Before I even got a chance to try out my garbled French, Anna told me that I'd lost my slot on Saturday morning; it also became apparent that my own show *Cheggers Plays Pop*, was go go, too. I was speechless and, needless to say, I didn't offer to go halves on the bill. Deep inside I knew that my career in children's TV was over. With a new head there are bound to be some changes, regardless of how high one's viewing figures were at the time. Recently she wrote a wonderful book in which she told people how I'd joined the BBC. There was no mention of how I got the boot.

Looking back, she was right. I was getting on a bit and it was time for me to move on. I'd stood still for so long it was time I found some work which was a little more exacting. But where?

I was in pantomime the same year, working with Geoff Capes in *Jack and the Bean Stalk*. I played the part of Simple Simon and he should have played the giant but instead took on the role of Little John, so that he'd have more to do in the show. Great part, wrong panto! The giant only appears in the last scene of the show and our employers thought it was unfair to make the audience wait for such a long time before seeing Geoff. We were in Lewisham fighting off the tough critics penning their criticisms of our performance from the auditorium. But they weren't as tough as the youngsters that sat beside them. From the stage we could see the young theatregoers chomping popcorn and opening sweet wrappers as well as beating hell out of each other when anyone sang a love song.

It was a dangerous place to be, not Lewisham, but anywhere on stage. Boiled sweets would be hurled at every thespian that came on. One night, the baddie leapt off stage and thirty Boy Scouts and twenty Brownies fell on top of him. Their one-liners were more succinct and sometimes funnier than our own. One little bastard from the audience handed me a note to read out as a birthday request. I, being the kids' favourite and wanting to be liked by all, read it out aloud. 'I've just been given a note here by a young chap who'd like me to say Happy Birthday to Mike Hunt', I said. 'Is he around, Mike Hunt? Mike Hunt, are you out there?' It slowly dawned on me what I was saying. If you say it quickly enough, as I did, the obscenity is quite clear. I have never been so embarrassed. All I could do was leave the stage promptly with a smile and a Cheggers chuckle.

I drank regularly in the mornings now, but I managed not to while in the theatre. As soon as the show was over, I was first in the pub across the road for three, four or more lagers with the rest of the cast. I was staying locally with my sister-in-law and on the way home I would stop off to buy a bottle of whisky. It was easy for me to drink with her around, as she would never suggest to me that I had a problem. She wasn't earning too much, so by paying her a bit of rent, buying her the odd meal and a glass of vino, I was giving her a bit of a treat.

Drink was beginning to affect me mentally. On many occasions I'd have to look at the script before going on stage as I genuinely couldn't remember the next scene. One night we had a party for the cast of another panto up the road. After the show was over, the cast assembled in a room at the back of the theatre for a bit of a bop and a booze-up. I had been guzzling since the curtain went down and was well and truly out of my tree by the time the other show members arrived. I must have been in blackout as I believe I went into my naughty disco cabaret mode and was asking people to take part in various risqué competitions. I was told the following day about my antics and, although they were just schoolboy practical jokes and pranks and nothing really to worry about, once again I couldn't remember a thing. That did worry me.

In December '88, before the panto's run had finished, I had an audition for a new television series on Sky television called *Star Search*. I got the job. The programme was made by the Australian production company Grundy Television, who also make programmes like *Neighbours* and *Prisoner: Cell Block H*. It was to be Sky's answer to *Opportunity Knocks* and bigger and better than *New Faces*. A talent show for the general public.

The show was made at the old London Weekend Television studios on the South Bank. This was a relatively new era of television where outside production companies would hire mainstream television facilities to make their own productions. I had the feeling that the British workforce who were appointed as our crew on the show weren't too keen on working with an Aussie production company. Some of the South Bank team were the old boys of television, the hard knocks school who knew the industry and everyone else's job inside out. They didn't mind speaking their minds and would never suck up to nambypamby producers and directors who were far more interested in making career moves with the artistes than knowing the ins and outs of real television.

I sussed within hours that this supposedly motley crew we'd been given were really the *crème de la crème* of television. Combined with an Australian production team who were hard as nails and one of the best directors in the country, it couldn't fail.

To the whole of the television industry's surprise, we managed to turn out five one-hour talent shows a day. It was an all-time record. Once the titles rolled we performed like a dream team. During the recording, so as not to stop the show in its flow, I would ad lib with extra pieces to the camera for the crew if they weren't set for the next act on the show; likewise they would cover for me. Nothing could stop us. Each programme was done live and, to this day, I have never worked with such dedicated professionals.

The show bragged the fact that no one failed the audition; and it was true, no one did. The real reason was that no one with any talent ever turned up. The show was on five nights a week and it wasn't long before we'd exhausted all the real talent in the country. The show had to resort to flying in the odd act from Europe to add that extra bit of sparkle in between the bad acts. We'd already invited back a lot of the artistes for repeat performances; some had been on the show three or four times. There was one chap who strictly speaking failed the audition, but he was so pissed the auditioning team couldn't even get a name or address out of him, let alone appreciate his act. But what a show it turned out to be! Viewing figures went Sky high and it turned out to be compulsive viewing. Two thousand acts graced the satellite viewers' screens and some were quite unique. We had them all. I introduced a young chap on the show with his act 'Robert's World of Magic'. He invited two members of the audience to tie him up in a sack which he would escape from in a matter of seconds. They tied him up and left him to his own devices. Three minutes later, he was still struggling to get free. Eventually, I had to walk in and cut him loose with a pen knife.

There were no edits in the show, so when people forgot their comedy routines or the lyrics to a song it all stayed. One comedian came on and his wig slipped; it was left in. Each act was judged and awarded points. One Italian opera singer was marked very low by

Suzy Quatro. A slanging match ensued in which the Italian opera singer said to Suzy, 'You no tell me how to sing. Your voice, you crap.' Right Said Fred appeared on the programme along with Chesney Hawkes, but the rest of the one thousand, nine hundred and ninety-eight are still trying to make it.

My spell with *Star Search* is the only television period of my life that I would wish to relive. More so than my days on *Swap Shop* or even *Cheggers Plays Pop*. We worked hard but we played hard, too. I would enjoy evenings after the show, heading to a small bar next door to party the rest of the night away with the crew. More than a few times I had to be carted out of the bar and into an awaiting car. It was my privilege and my treat for working so hard, to let my hair down.

There was a sort of end of term party which had been organised for us at Joe Allen's restaurant in London. One could always guarantee meeting a pop or film star at the next table. I got there early and ordered a double Scotch. A couple of tables away I smiled at Tyne Daley from *Cagney and Lacey*. I thought about asking for her autograph, but I was too embarrassed.

By the time the rest of the team arrived, I was well ahead of the party. I didn't even enquire as to who was drinking red or white wine, as I guzzled everything that came to the table.

Eventually puddings were placed on the table, followed by my head. I'm not too sure what happened next, but I believe I was carried out of the restaurant and dumped into a cab. In total blackout, I headed for the South Bank and London Weekend Television studios to visit the rest of my mates.

I don't know how I made it home that night, but I had a phone call from a member of the crew the following morning who was very concerned about my welfare. I lied and bragged about the great night we'd all had together and he filled me in on what went on. He told me I was loud, a bit of a laugh and had collected quite a large crowd at the bar by the end of the evening telling them a selection of anecdotes and dirty gags. All the drinks had been on me and my Barclaycard. Twenty-six bottles of champagne and an open tab behind the bar later and I still can't remember much about it.

Blackouts would come and go. One night I'd stop before going over my limit, which was about three-quarters of a bottle, the next I'd start my second and keel over till the morning.

Meanwhile, television work came in dribs and drabs. One month I'd record forty *Star Search* shows for Sky TV and then I'd do nothing for three. I was forced to become a professional guest and appeared on all the celebrity game shows. Not having to present a programme gave me the chance to relax. It meant that I could have half a lager before recording a show. But if I really needed to shape up for a major job, I'd stop the day before so I would be in what I thought at the time was top form. Without really being aware of it, I was finding it hard to work. I had problems concentrating, I started to use notes and crib cards and I developed new ways of tackling my job which went hand in hand with my drinking. I would stay in a hotel the night before the show so that I was free to help myself to the mini bar. In the morning I would settle that part of the account myself and even tell the receptionist I'd had a few people from the show back for drinks, hence such a heavy bar bill.

If it wasn't possible to stay overnight, I would insist on the TV company paying my driver to shuttle me from location to location so I could sleep en route. Even my driver became part of the drinking plan. I'd say goodbye to my producer friends and relish the moment I got into the car as my chauffeur had bought in the beers for me to drink on the way home. I would down half a bottle of whisky, sleep most of the journey and wake up just before I got home, fresh as a daisy. I amazed my driver with my ability to drink so much so quickly, sleep and then appear to be stone cold sober immediately afterwards.

I was on a learning curve. I was teaching myself ways to handle my booze. I was playing with the chemicals: too much too quickly and I'd blackout: a little and often was just right.

As time and my addiction progressed, everything else got worse. The simple idea of going out for an evening with friends appalled me. I did not want their company. They'd just get in the way of my drinking. I would have to resort to desperate measures, secretly taking half bottles of Scotch with me for emergencies. If I felt a need for a top-up during my time with them, I'd pop out to the car on the pretence of getting some fags and have a swig from my secret supply. If plates at the dinner table were to be cleared, I'd be the first to offer my services, knowing that there would be that half bottle of wine in the kitchen that I could down quickly, unbeknown to my hosts at the table.

I hated the weekends, in particular Sunday, Bloody Sunday. Have you ever tried to buy a bottle before midday or after two on a Sunday? Your big supermarkets have signs up saying you can't buy alcohol till twelve. Your local shop can't sell it because they might lose their licence. So you have to sit there watching the clock slowly ticking by. I imagined all these alcoholics, like football fans ready to invade the pitch. As soon as the clock chimes twelve, they converge on off licences all over the country. Can you imagine what the computers for Visa and Access must be going through? If I owned Threshers, I'd sit there in front of my computer console watching my stock go down and my bank balance go up.

One Sunday, I was invited to lunch with a couple of people, so bang went my trip to the off licence. What's more, I had no secret supplies. I was desperate. When I arrived I was offered some hot punch. As I was being given the glass, my eyes went straight to the pan it had come from. There wasn't enough there to keep me going for the afternoon. I swung round to admire their kitchen, but really I was on a top secret mission, recce-ing the joint for open bottles and supplies. I'd need more than a couple of hot toddies to stop me shaking and sweating.

By the time lunch was served, I wasn't feeling too good. I struggled to make conversation, but my mind was elsewhere. As was the norm at this sort of social gathering, there was one bottle of red and one bottle of white wine on the table and the host had positioned the bottles near himself. Before we sat down I headed for a seat nearest the drink, but I was directed to another chair at the end of the table. After pudding, plates were being removed from the table. My offer to help clear away the dishes had been turned down twice, but I had to make a move. I got up from the table and headed with a dirty dish towards the kitchen. When I got there I saw half a bottle of red wine on one of the work surfaces. I waited for the right moment. When the hostess went into the dining room, I seized the golden opportunity to consume what was left in the bottle. I was like a fish as I had developed the art of swigging down pints in a matter of seconds during my lager and real ale days. Only recently, I was challenged on this matter and battled it out with a mate drinking pints of water. Naturally, I won.

On my hostess's return, she quizzed me about the empty bottle. I said I thought it was finished and had poured it down the sink. Once again Lady Luck was with me. In fact, throughout my drinking period someone was looking after me.

At about that time I thought about going to my GP for some help. I kept putting off the idea because the surgery I belonged to then was very anti-smoking – they came at you like sniffer dogs blaming everything from haemorrhoids to hernias, sties to cystitis, even the loss of a limb on smoking. Anyway, I wanted to talk about the strange symptoms I was now experiencing without them finding out that they were all possibly down to my excessive consumption of booze. So I decided to do some medical research of my own.

First and foremost, I wanted to find out what alcohol was doing to my body. I went to all my local book shops, searching high and low for something that would immediately give me that information – but to no avail. There was nothing and I certainly wasn't going to ask for a book on booze. 'Excuse me, I believe I may be drinking too much. Do you have any material in your reference section relating to whether I'm a pisshead or not?' I found a few books with the words 'alcoholic' and 'drinker' plastered all over the front cover, but I wasn't going to walk out of the shop with the embarrassment of people looking at me and thinking that I had a problem. Can you imagine walking out of a book shop with a cover entitled *Piles and How to Handle Them* or *Learning How to Live with Flatulence*? No bloody way would anyone want to stand in a queue with any one of those under their arm, so how can you expect a drinker who wants to give up to do the same?

There were some medical books which had a single complicated section on alcohol and its effects but there was nothing that told me why I had pains in my back and the rest of my body. Why I suffered bouts of dry vomiting without a moment's notice. Why I was shaking, sweating and having panic attacks. I wanted to know whether drink was affecting my brain and, more importantly, was I going to die if I carried on?

There were plenty of good reads from sober fellow celebrities with their life stories, which would include the odd anecdote or funny drinking story. Then there were the heavy mob who suggested either finding God or solving one's drinking problem with a stiff walk rather than a stiff half. I wasn't looking for page after page of elaborate information, I just wanted a simple guide to how to stop drinking.

One weekend I was out touring antiques shops in Marlborough, Wiltshire. I'd been given a copy of *Lyle Antiques Price Guide* by a friend; heaven knows why. I was no Arthur Negus and if *The Antiques Road Show* came on TV, I popped out to have a drink in private, while everyone else watched it. However, I had decided to use this gift to surprise my friend by buying some priceless artefact. After looking through the book and studying its form, I was convinced that the owners of these little shops didn't have a clue what real treasures lay inches from their grasp.

Needless to say, I didn't find a priceless antique, but I did come across the odd tatty book section. In one of these I found a medical book dating back to the turn of the century. As I fumbled through its pages, I found a section on alcohol – three pages of waffle about how it is absorbed into the body and what you can do with it, but only a few sentences relating to me. I quote from *The Universal Home Doctor*: 'Alcohol supplies energy to the body and may thus be considered a food'. That was good enough for me! A food. Bloody brilliant. I was starving.

CHAPTER FOUR

By the end of June 1991 my drinking was, to say the least, getting worse and as time went by I was becoming more and more secretive. I was also being nagged by those around me. Maggie, Maria and even close friends were always mentioning my excessive drinking; they seemed to watch my every move. Maggie even had the cheek to suggest that I sometimes smelt of booze and that I had been drinking during the day.

Maggie seemed to be getting a little tired of coming home to find me asleep on the sofa. I'd wake up and make some excuse about overworking or not sleeping the night before. But it was Maria who I felt knew the real truth. She'd see me pop out to the shops for something and I'm sure she knew it wasn't just a packet of fags. She could not say too much as she never actually caught me in the act. Even if she had, it wouldn't have been a wise move to accuse the boss of drinking, as I would have made sure her departure from our house wasn't long after.

I used to use all sorts of elaborate techniques to smuggle booze into the house. I'd hide it inside an overcoat, slide a bottle into the back of my trousers and wear a short jacket to conceal the bump. I'd hide it inside the engine of my car, down the backs of seats and alongside the spare wheel for collection and consumption later. One of my other wheezes was to conceal several bottles round the garden, in privet hedges, down holes and in trees. I'd even put it in the guttering – half a bottle fitted quite nicely into the gutter's semicircular moulding. I'd also shove it down my long socks and once I walked with it in the hood of my Barbour jacket.

I was lucky enough to have created my own space in my recording studio. It was situated well away from the main house, which allowed me to drink in private. People couldn't be bothered to make the extra effort to walk across the yard to have a chat or bring me a cuppa. The studio was a bit like Aladdin's cave. If Lord Caernarvon was allowed to perform one of his archaeological digs he'd have found a treasure trove of delights: Golden Bells (Scotch whisky), Amber (bottles of cider) and quite a few cans of Double Diamond. Bottles were hidden everywhere. I even spent some time building secret panels to hide my stash on either side of my mixing desk which only I knew how to remove. Once in a while when no one else was around I'd have a clear-out and get rid of all my empty bottles. I distributed them around the area in other people's dustbins, a couple here and a couple there.

It wasn't so easy to drink during the day when there was a chance of being caught, so most of my drinking was done late in the evening and in the secure surroundings of my studio. I was boozing so heavily at nights that some mornings my head was so far down the loos you'd have thought I was a rep for Dyno-Rod. I became the Jacques Cousteau of the bog. If ever I was asked to go on *Mastermind* my chosen subject would have to be toilet seats, bowls and cisterns from 1987 to 1992. Twyford, Trent, Armitage Shanks, I got to know them all intimately. I'd also mastered the art of the silent heave. If I was to pop into some else's bathroom, I'd use either a towel, the arm of a dressing gown or a mate's coat to cover my mouth and nose and retch in muffled silence. Then at the very last moment I'd position my head over the bowl and throw up.

I avoided driving at all costs. I didn't want to use my car for fear of being stopped by the police. I had already taken the precaution of hiring a chauffeur to drive me to work, but I needed something to get me around locally, so I bought a mountain bike on which I could cycle to the off licence under the pretence of getting fit and healthy. I was not one for half measures. If something was to be done, I had to do it properly. I wasn't the sort of guy to make do with a tatty old push bike. I bought a top of the range Raleigh mountain bike with twenty-one gears. My bike had all mod cons, including a speedometer which also doubled as a temperature gauge and clock. One piddly light at the front and one at the back of the bike wasn't good enough for me – I had two lots of halogen bulbs at the front and two stop lights for the back. I kitted myself out in the full cycle gear: black and red non-slip leather gloves with air holes so my hands could breathe, an aerodynamically tested crash helmet designed to offer little air resistance when my head was stooped over the handle bars, a slim fitting cycling singlet complete with designer logo and a pair of cycling shorts with sewn-in padded chamois leather seat.

The planning that went into the shortest of rides was done with military precision. I had a backpack, which contained a selection of wet weather gear, a rubber torch and a fluorescent vest. I had an emergency tool kit tied to the cross bar containing screwdrivers, spanners, pliers and emergency equipment. Strapped next to that was a first aid kit and, if that wasn't enough, I would take with me two bottles of liquid refreshment to drink en route. All this to go and get a drink. But the effort, I thought, was worth it. Rain, hail or shine, I'd pedal through the Berkshire countryside giving the impression I was cycling for exercise. I'd breeze into my local shop to buy a paper and a pint of milk and during my conversation with the shopkeeper add to my shopping list a bottle of whisky.

On my return from the shops, I couldn't wait to get down the road and stop to have a guzzle. But one day I stopped once too often, polished off the entire contents of my precious bottle and blacked out. The next thing I remember was waking up in a hedge on the side of the road with a motorist enquiring about my welfare. He thought I'd been hit by a passing vehicle and thrown off my bike into the roadside. I scrambled out of the hedgerow and in gobbledy gook explained that I'd had rather a long cycle and was having a little nap. I was covered in hawthorn scratches and looked like some masochistic camper. I didn't make it home till after dark that night; apparently there had been expedition parties sent out in search of me and my mountain bike. I was quizzed about where I'd been and the condition I was in, in particular the torn clothing and scratches on my body. I think I just about got away with the excuse that I'd been for a very long ride and came a cropper while doing a bit of off-roading when my brakes jammed and I went over the handle bars. I also explained that because of a buckled front wheel I'd had to walk home. Phew!

Every day that passed I'd have to emulate Tony Slattery, the master of ad lib and improvisation. If I was given a problem I'd have to react quickly using rapid wit and inventiveness. Day in, day out I'd create the most ridiculous stories.

On one occasion I was desperate for a drink, but the only alcohol in the house was a special gift-wrapped bottle of malt whisky complete with presentation case. I hadn't attempted to open it before as it was a corked bottle with a lead seal which, if tampered with, would result in me being found out as the guilty party. But on that occasion I took on the presentation lead seal corked bottle that had eluded me for so long.

I've never been much of a patient person. I hate anything like painting or model making as the end result takes too long to accomplish. That is probably why I admire painters like Rolf Harris and the modern artists – a flick of a brush or a few bricks stacked at random is quickly achieved. I couldn't have been someone like Constable, who must have spent days painting a blade of grass. If I'd been given the job of painting the Sistine Chapel, it would have been done in a couple of hours. No need for all that scaffolding, just chuck a few buckets of whitewash on the ceiling, add a few splodges of colour and Bob's your uncle.

Taking on the challenge of the bottle was not easy. I studied its shape, the way it was wrapped and how to tackle the removal of the cork and lead seal. I was like a bomb disposal expert. My task took over two hours to perform. The lead seal came off a treat, but the cork proved to be the most time-consuming. I had to work slowly using a long darning needle. Slowly but surely the cork came out unscathed by my relentless gentle probing. Then I removed the contents and replaced it with cold tea. Only recently did I tell people about this escapade.

By the way, the only bottle in the house that I didn't consume was a quarter bottle of champagne I was given when my daughter was born. You'd have thought a pisshead like me would have guzzled it without thinking, but no, for some unknown reason, it still has its genuine contents, although my fingerprints must be all over it.

By now, if a presenting job came in, I had got working my drinking around the job off to a tee. A day before any television commitment I'd start drinking Night Nurse. I found that it held back the withdrawal symptoms from alcohol for a short period. It would allow me to get my act together and help restrain the shakes, sweating and dry vomiting. But not for long. Once the job was finished I'd be back on to the drug of my choice and, hey presto, no one was the wiser. Clever bastard. It would be absurd of any of my colleagues to suggest to me or anyone else that I had a drink problem.

Each morning, unbeknown to anyone, I'd wake up like a deck chair that had been in storage all winter and was being opened for the first time in months. I was in need of more than a few squirts of WD40 to get me going, though. Most mornings I'd slide to the floor of my bedroom and wait for my torso to unravel.

A lot of the time I was in agony, because of the untold damage I was doing to my body through heavy drinking. The mornings were a minefield of confusion. Where had I been? What had I been doing? Had I wet the bed? Thrown up on the floor? I'd look around the room for clues of the previous evening's activity. What was I wearing? Was I still wearing it?

Then I'd stagger painfully to my second home the bathroom and examine my body in the mirror. There I could see the usual array of bruising from taking falls in my drunken stupor, a colourful mixture of dark blue interspersed with splashes of amber and yellow. Were there any extra marks or blemishes where maybe I'd fallen the night before? I looked like I'd been playing paint gun games and forgotten to put on a protective overall. My eyes were red, my face was puffed out and my body was yellow. I was playing mind games. What the fuck happened last night? Frankly, I hadn't a clue.

I couldn't face up to the truth. I was more at ease with the excuse that all my ailments were caused by some bug going round or that my diarrhoea was due to eating a bad pasty. I was spending a lot of time in the downstairs loo. It became a bit of a joke for others, but for me it was sheer hell. I prepared for my morning chat with God on the big white telephone by taking with me my coffee, fags and lighter and an extra bog roll to save shouting for a refill. It was awful. Some mornings I wasn't sure whether to stand up or sit down. I can only describe what happened as pouring booze in one end and it coming out the other. I had dry vomiting that seemed to go on for ages, I coughed blood and I had pains in my back and more. All of this, I hasten to add, had to be done in silence for fear of people asking too many questions. I told no one about my morning marathon and no one suspected anything; they'd got used to the idea that I would spend longer than anyone else in the bathroom. Thank heavens we had two toilets. By the time I'd finished in one, you could have had a coach party of pensioners through the other. Throughout all this, I still continued to drink.

Within three heavy years of drinking, my addiction to alcohol was full blown. All my desperate mind and body wanted was to get a drink and, having got one, to keep it down without throwing up. I still believed I had total control over my drinking but, by now, it had full control of me. Shaking, sweating, vomiting and diarrhoea were part of everyday life. Panic attacks when I couldn't get a drink were severe. Friends, family and work were an easy second choice to my drinking. I stunk of booze and had every excuse in the book at hand in case I was quizzed. 'You smell of drink.' 'Didn't get in till late. What a party!' 'You sweat a lot.' 'I think I've got a touch of the 'flu coming on.'

The lies grew bigger and I became more deceptive as time went by. Still I got progressively worse. My family tried to help by coming to stay and keep an eye on me if Maggie was away working but, to be honest, they just got in the bloody way, spoiling my routine. I became a master of deceit and after two days I'd convince them that I was perfectly all right. When they left, thank God, I could return to my closest friend at that time, the bottle.

I was always contemplating trying to stop for the umpteenth time. I remember lying in bed with a tumbler full of whisky knowing I was killing myself. I didn't want a life like this any more. I finished my tumbler and blacked out. Giving up was such a big hurdle, like trying to jump Becher's Brook on a Shetland pony. I knew that if I could get over that first jump I might have a chance. I had to do something, and quickly.

I eventually plucked up enough courage to admit to Maggie that I thought I might have a problem. I didn't tell her everything, just enough for her to agree to come with me to see my doctor. I thought that by taking Maggie with me I would make her and Maria think that I was prepared to do something about it.

I told my doctor as much as I wanted to. He was unlike the other doctors in the practice. The others were making all the right moves, but their minds seemed to be in other places. It was a change to be asked to sit down and talk about my condition and what I was going through. He groped various parts of my anatomy and took a blood test. He also suggested that I meet a specialist who helps people with drinking problems who could give me some advice as to what steps I should take next.

Days later this expert arrived at the house for a chat. He certainly looked the part: smart suit, white shirt and tie and black bag. He spoke with eloquence and in depth about alcohol and its effects and quizzed me on my thoughts on the matter. After an hour or so, he gave me his opinion. He suggested that I stop drinking heavy spirits and try wine or lager. What planet was he on? Here was I desperately wanting to stop and he was telling me to get it down with a funnel if necessary.

Maggie had been witness to his expertise and guidance and was content to let me continue to drink providing it was white wine or lager. I was so grateful for the opportunity to come out of the closet for a while, but little did she know that I exceeded the boundaries of his limitations by topping up my white wine bottle with vodka and the lager can with whisky. It was my version of controlled drinking and one which was working wonders for me.

Two weeks into my controlled drinking routine and uncontrollability took over. I was back to blacking out, throwing up, bed wetting and drinking sometimes two bottles of whisky a day.

I remember waking up one morning and telling myself this was the day. This was the day I was going to stop. I made plans to remove all the empty bottles and secret supplies from inside and outside the house. But my body was aching, it felt like it needed a drink. It was already asking for its morning fix. I was late in responding, so it started to remind me every five sodding minutes. Tremors shot through me. It felt like someone had poked my arse, testicles, head, arms and legs with a pitch fork. I sweated and vomited and panicked all at once. The fits went on without remorse. One minute I was freezing cold, the next sweat came pouring out of my body as though I'd just run a marathon. I tried to sleep but I woke up in a frenzy every time. I was having one of my panic attacks. They were so real. It was a living nightmare – anything from being eaten alive by flies, to the fear of going outside the house in case someone saw me. I had a continual feeling of claustrophobia as though someone had put me in a straitjacket and I was desperate to get out. I prayed to God that He would take all this away, but He didn't.

Three days were as much as I could take. I couldn't eat. I'd struggle with a bowl of soup and then it would come back like Gandhi's revenge. The dry vomiting continued. I was drinking water and then pissing it out orange. My body was getting rid of all its impurities.

I remember phoning another doctor from the same surgery to see if he could help me get through the night with some medication. No such luck. He casually told me that it was my fault for drinking too much. Bastard.

I phoned Alcoholics Anonymous. I had very little to say, but the chap on the end of the phone coaxed me away from drink for another few hours by telling me his story and what he had to go through to stop. It wasn't too dissimilar to mine. I asked him about controlled drinking and clinics. He didn't advocate the 'glass of wine will be fine' routine, but he thought a clinic might help me sort myself out. It was obvious that if I didn't do something soon, I'd be wrapped round a bottle within only a few hours of putting the phone down.

Maggie was away at the time. She had gone to Leicester with Rose to see her parents. I think that this time she had really had enough of me and my drinking. I wanted to sort myself out.

I asked Maria to get in touch with some places that deal with alcohol abuse. To my amazement, they're not hard to come by, they're all there in the Yellow Pages under the heading 'Clinics'. Some go as far as block advertising. I immediately thought 'expensive'. Maybe if I wanted to back out at the last minute I could use this as an excuse to continue drinking. I'd tell everyone I'd love to go but I seriously couldn't afford it. I also wondered whether I could breeze in and out of a clinic without anyone noticing. I was so worried that my whereabouts would be leaked to the press. I could just imagine the headline: 'Cheggers drinks more than his pop'. In one way I was merely another celebrity drying out, but I knew I would be singled out because of my unscathed image as a children's TV presenter. I remember the press having a field day with a former children's presenter who was photographed dancing in a night club in some raunchy leather gear. What would they do to me?

Maria spoke to a clinic which shall remain anonymous, but for the purposes of this book I will call Chesterton Grange. It is a clinic that helps addicts of all kinds and is probably one of the best in the country. As well as helping people give up their addictions it also looked after psychiatric patients.

I remember the phone call vividly. Maria had detailed instructions from me to ask what I thought were relevant questions. Is there a TV with remote control in every room? Do you have a swimming pool, sauna or jacuzzi? Is there a snooker room or pool table? And, top of the list, can you smoke? If I was to give up drinking I was going to do it in style.

Very sensibly, Maria asked none of these questions but made up a few of her own. What can you do to help him? What medical treatment and supervision will he get? She went into the ins and outs of the clinic and how it worked as I sat by listening and pushing my list in front of her to no avail. The phone went down and it was decision time for me. Maria made no attempt to encourage or discourage me. It had to be my decision. I had seen a film once in which a guy was slung into a loony bin for drinking, he was tied to a bed and made to go through withdrawal symptoms without medical help. I imagined myself shackled to a Victorian bed, bathed in sweat and going cold turkey alone while doctors and friends watched over me and told me it was all my fault. You shouldn't have picked up that bottle, you've only yourself to blame.

Maria spoke to one of the counsellors at the clinic. He guaranteed that I would be in safe hands. The staff were used to dealing with celebrities and my stay there would be in total confidence. Neither he nor his workforce would leak anything to the press. Total anonymity was their motto. Their main concern was my welfare and he assured Maria that my every need, if I truly wanted to give up, would be catered for. Mind you, at the prices he charged, he was bound to sell the virtues of his country home for drunks. He probably also sold time share deals, I thought, and gave away a free telly if you stayed for more than six weeks.

I had to find a lot of money to go there. I was pretty broke so I even contemplated selling my much-treasured Land Rover. What a car! The Landie had seen me through hell and back. It was a 3.5 litre short wheel base with tow bar, intermittent windscreen wipers and air conditioning (basically, the faster I drove it, the more the air rushed through the gaps in the doors). It was my pride and joy. I had bought it after I went on the programme *Jim'll Fix It* to give a couple of people the chance to test drive a Land Rover over an arduous obstacle course in the West Midlands. I was so impressed by its performance that I'd bought it there and then – an ex-demo model at a reduced price. It wasn't everyone's idea of a celebrity car. When I turned up to open a shop or a fête, the Land Rover came too. I was once asked if my other car had broken down. I informed the rather snotty enquirer that it was my only car and I was proud of it. He then promptly asked me to park it round the back.

For the moment, though, I could use some cash I was saving for the taxman in my building society. The Land Rover could stay in the drive a little longer as I contemplated the thought of going into the clinic. My mum and dad had arrived during the afternoon along with my sister Janice and Paul, Janice's partner. They were on my side. They had no worries about leaks to the press. They weren't concerned about how neighbours, relatives or even workmates would react. Their only concern was me. They'd seen me at my best, without the booze, and now they were confronted with me at my worst.

I decided to give it a go. I had tried everything else, doctors, controlled drinking and self help, but nothing had worked, and going it alone was always disastrous.

Maria phoned the clinic to let them know I was on my way. I could imagine their thoughts, 'Bloody hell, not Cheggers', six weeks of Britain's biggest prat. I crept upstairs on the pretence of packing my bags and went straight to my wardrobe, where I had half a bottle of whisky hidden in a suit jacket. I remember standing in my walk-in wardrobe guzzling the last dregs of what was going to be my last binge. As I drank I had the pleasure of thinking that if they're gonna cure me, they may as well start from scratch.

I could hear Janice darting up the stairs. Isn't it amazing how agile some people can be? She came up those stairs like Sally Gunnell, but I too had developed some amazing skills during my drinking. I screwed the top back on the empty bottle and slung it, like a contestant on *Bull's Eye*, back into the inside pocket of the suit it came from and counted the seconds before she appeared in the room.

Janice assured me that she'd visit me in the clinic and with that I started to pack a bag. Maria agreed to drive me there and before I knew it I was kissing everyone goodbye and on my way.

CHAPTER FIVE

I slept for most of the journey, only waking up when we got to the driveway of Chesterton Grange. It was 1 November 1991. There was a dark and eerie glow from the building's outside light which cast long shadows. The place had a touch of class. It was a Queen Anne house in an area where you're talking mega bucks to live in a semi.

Maria left me in the car and went inside to let them know I'd arrived. I was helped in by a male nurse with a Liverpudlian accent. Why is it that whenever I meet fellow Scousers I feel that any minute they're going to try and sell me something or tap me for a few bob? I hasten to add that he didn't. The reception area was a bit like a hotel lobby. There was a reception desk, but no sign of a receptionist. There was a leather couch and flowers decorated the tables. I was most impressed by the array of flora until I saw, hanging from each bouquet, thank you cards. Obviously donated by patients who'd left and wanted to show their appreciation for a great stay. When you've spent thousands of pounds on treatment, I thought, what's the odd fifty quid for a bunch of flowers?

I was shown to my room. It was very large, which didn't suit the single bed in it, with huge shuttered windows overlooking the grounds. There was a small bathroom, a phone, but no television. The least said the better, I thought. I would pursue this matter once I was better acquainted with the people working there.

I was in the room for no more than a few minutes when I asked if I was allowed to smoke. The instruction came back as quickly as the question was uttered. There was to be no smoking in the bedrooms, but if I was gasping for a fag then there was a lounge designated for smokers downstairs. During the next few weeks I was to see more of that room than the view from my bedroom window. Maria and I were left alone for a few minutes. We spoke in whispers. I was so paranoid that I thought the room may be bugged, or that there was someone earholing outside the door.

My guardian for the evening returned and went through the entire contents of my bag. Each item was noted and the odd thing was taken away. Lighter fuel, mouthwash and even a sachet of Lemsip were removed. I was asked a whole load of questions about my health. My replies were totally honest, all of them bar one, that is. 'When did you last have a drink?' I thought about it for a few moments grabbing back all those years of stage school when I was requested to improvise thought, confusion and dilemma in an instant. I thought I'd performed all three pretty competently and told the quiz master that my last drink had been a few days ago. All my acting was spoilt, however, by Maria the heckler, who let loose that I'd just finished half a bottle. How did she know?

A doctor arrived with a Doolittle bag to give me a medical examination. He was a local chap who was brought in from outside the clinic to assess my health and to make sure I wasn't going to collapse that night. I had the feeling when he was giving me the once over that he was non-plussed by the shape I was in. I'm sure he could smell booze.

He leant over me a few more times than I would have liked. At one time, I thought he was going to kiss me. He left and told me I would be given something later to help me sleep and keep calm. I knew it wasn't going to be a drink, but I had this silly thought I was going to be given a hot chocolate and then whacked over the back of the head with a baseball bat.

I was given a guided tour, which took no more than a couple of minutes. There was a dining room, a long conference room with a ping pong table and piano, a non-smoking room and a smoking room. That was it. No jacuzzi, no snooker table and no sign of a swimming pool. I was not a happy man. It had already been a blow not having a television, but a TV was a small request compared to asking them if they could ship in a whole leisure centre. During our very short walk I noticed a shortage of clientele and thought that maybe some had already retired for the evening due to boredom.

It was time for Maria to leave. I walked her to the car and we said our goodbyes. At this point I felt very vulnerable. As the car pulled away I wondered whether to chase after it. I even contemplated checking out of the clinic. I didn't want to be left on my own with a bunch of strangers. It was then that I looked over my shoulder and saw my Liverpudlian mate keeping an eye on me.

When I was back inside he said that he wasn't too sure whether I should mix with the other patients as I smelt of booze. I must have looked a rather sorry picture as he eventually agreed to let me watch TV downstairs, as there was not one in my room. I headed straight for the smoking room.

It was a small lounge with a large television and a few leather sofas that had seen better days. The ceiling was heavily tarred with cigarette smoke and the lighting was dark and dingy, a bit like a pub. I lit up a fag and had a chat with a very cheerful Scots lad who told me he was also a newcomer. The conversation was very one-sided, to be honest, as I wasn't in the mood for conversation. I could feel the subject was about to swing round to the question 'Are you Keith Chegwin?' I made an excuse and popped outside for some fresh air. An innocent venture on my part, but one which I hear caused quite a lot of distress to the staff. New patients are not allowed outside without supervision or permission during their first few days. While I was casually lighting up in the garden and peering up at the stars, the entire workforce were playing *The Hunt for Red October*. Only when I went back inside was I made aware of the house rules.

Back in the smoking room I wondered when this very expensive treatment would start. The effects of the recently consumed alcohol were wearing off and I started to feel tense and nervous. What's more, the shakes were returning. I was sweating quite a lot and about the last thing I wanted to do was talk. I was asked by one of the patients what I was in for. I thought I should have replied with something suitable for a prison term – armed robbery, GBH or fraud perhaps. I held back my reply and informed him I was in for a while. Sounded a bit rude but, who knows, I could have been talking to the *News of the World* or he could have been one of the clinic's counsellors giving me a test. Or just some nosy bastard. It turned out that this particular inmate was seeking help for agoraphobia. He almost bragged to me that he was the only patient in the clinic allowed outside the grounds without supervision. From the way he was acting, I had a feeling he wouldn't make it past the reception desk.

A nurse appeared at my side and offered me a couple of tablets. Without enquiring as to what they were, I downed them quickly. I later found out they were sedatives to help me relax.

It took some time for the pills to work, but gradually I felt slightly more at ease and less anxious.

The rest of the evening was spent in the smoking room having the odd chat during commercial breaks on the television. I couldn't even tell you what was showing on TV that night. I just wanted to be left alone. But having been told that I couldn't smoke in my bedroom, my only option was to stay put. A couple of hours slipped by and my thoughts led inevitably to drink. That half bottle hadn't been enough and its effects weren't going to get me to sleep. I sat there contemplating my predicament, feeling very sorry for myself and the situation I had got myself into. I decided to go back to my room and lie down.

On my way upstairs I noticed that people, like insects, had crawled out of the woodwork. They were all congregated in the reception area. I decided to hang on for a bit. Maybe it was cabaret time or the fire alarm had gone off without my hearing it. Then I saw a trolley being wheeled in by two nurses. They opened the cabinet and began to dish out medical cocktails to the masses that had gathered. It was quite a social event. People bragged about how many tablets they were going to take that night. Some bragged about how few they were to receive. And one chap had one hell of an argument with the nurse about how he'd been diddled out of taking his full quota. I was just about to leave when my name was called. I was given yet another dose of pills and once again I didn't enquire as to what they were. If I'm spending all this money, I thought, I'll take everything you've got.

I went to my room and stared out of the bedroom window. A yellow glow came up from ground level illuminating the house, grounds and my bedroom. I wondered if it would keep me awake. I was feeling rather drowsy and my mouth felt like a wrestler's jockstrap. I needed to clean my teeth and thought about having a shower, but I couldn't be bothered. I didn't make it to the bathroom, I fell asleep.

I woke up in the early hours of the morning in a state of panic. I was totally disorientated; I was shaking, sweating and I felt sick. I tossed and turned in my bed and eventually got up to have a cigarette out of the window. It calmed me down a bit but I felt awful. I was dizzy and I could only presume it was the tablets that were affecting me so greatly. I staggered to the bathroom and started to heave. One minute I was calling for Hughie and the next I was playing musical chairs. I won a seat every time as the world fell out of my bottom.

Downstairs in the dining room tea and coffee were on the go twenty-four hours a day from a very upmarket vending machine. I decided to check it out, despite the hour. Looking at the array of buttons to choose from, I thought I was on Challenger One in charge of the shuttle space mission. It was just a pity that the coffee was that bloody filter variety. I've always been an instant man myself. A good cup of Gold Blend. I used to be a fan of Nescafé until Gareth Hunt and Sarah Greene started to do the advertising campaign for it. They'd stand in doorways, kitchens and living rooms shaking coffee beans in their hands. The impression I got from the advert, was that it was coffee for tossers.

All was quiet in the smoking room; just me and the smell of stale cigarettes. I heard a few noises from outside the room. It was the early morning kitchen staff preparing breakfast. I hadn't eaten for some time but the thought of food made me heave. I was having a bad time and it was obvious the pills they'd administered the night before had started to wear off. Then I was off again, like an Olympic athlete, the finishing line being the toilet seat. I made it, and the old dry vomiting started. Heave after heave produced nothing. I had diarrhoea, heaven knows where that was coming from. I felt dizzy and thought I might pass out. I wondered whether I should speak to one of the nurses, but I didn't want to make a fuss, draw attention to myself, so I thought better of it and decided not to bother anyone.

I must have been in the loo for a while, as by the time I returned to the smoking room it had filled up with people watching the television and reading the morning papers. They must have thought me odd as I made an about turn in the doorway and headed to the reception area to ask for permission to go outside. Again I wanted to be on my own.

Opposite the reception area was a sort of nursing station with a huge glass window. From where I stood it looked like a giant fish tank. I expected Jaws or a frogman to appear any minute. I've no idea how it had escaped my notice on the way in. It was a bit like going to Egypt and not seeing a pyramid. Through the glass I could see three or four nurses chatting to one another. The nurses didn't wear uniforms, but some wore name badges to distinguish themselves from the alkies, druggies and nutters in their care. Some may have forgotten to put them on or were too senior to wear them. I reckon it's the same as when some celebrities making personal appearances or doing the odd shop opening refuse to wear name tags or even security passes, as they think the world and his wife already know who they are.

Behind the glass was a small room. Typical Keith Chegwin, I waited patiently for a long while until someone saw me, then I requested to go outside. There was a lot of umming and ahhing and a bit of eyebrow twitching between the nurses on duty. I wondered whether a question on sport would have been easier.

There were not a lot of nurses to go round and definitely none keen enough to come outside and hold my hand in a freezing cold garden. Eventually, after much debate, permission was granted and I was allowed out, but only if I sat on the garden bench directly outside the dining room window, so they could keep an eye on me.

As I left reception I heard a long menacing scream let rip from somewhere upstairs. I forgot my pending engagement with the outside world and decided to stick around to see what would happen next. As I looked around, life carried on as normal. People were heading for breakfast and a queue was forming for the pill trolley. Maybe my preconceptions of being tied to a bed and left to sweat it out were a reality. That's why no one turned a hair. It was the norm at the clinic to hear the occasional scream, the odd wail of agony as a patient went cold turkey. I headed for the garden.

It was a cold, crisp November morning. A few early birds were foraging around and the sun was out. The gardens were well established – good thick hedges and gravelled paths that seemed to go on for miles. It reminded me of the film *The Secret Garden* and I wondered at this point whether there was a secret way out. But I obeyed my orders and sat on the bench outside the dining room. I lit a fag and thought, Where the fuck am I? I had been out cold on the way here, and I wasn't sure whether we'd done a left on to the M4 motorway from Newbury or a right. If we'd gone left, I could be anywhere between Newbury and Wales. If we'd turned right, I could be anywhere in Great Britain. The nearby door swung open and a nurse enquired as to my welfare. I assured her I was OK, although I wasn't, and off she went about her business. Five minutes later, another nurse repeated the same exercise and ten minutes later yet another. It was a bit like a Brian Rix farce, doors banging and one-liners being exchanged. I was waiting for the vicar and the voluptuous blonde in high heels and stockings to burst through the doors any second. I thought it best to return to the smoking room and face some of the other patients.

I got talking to an elderly lady who seemed to be a regular at Chesterton Grange. She told me she had been to the clinic on many occasions to recuperate after the various hospital operations she'd had. The surgeon's scalpel seemed to have removed many a vital organ from her body and she appeared to relish the opportunity to relive her experiences with me. It was more like a chat with a musketeer as she described all the cut and thrust. By the end of our conversation, which echoed round the entire room, I was pretty sure that people on their way to breakfast would not be having the kidneys. Our conversation got round to the weekends at the clinic. She told me that not much happened then as weekends were a time to digest and reflect on what had gone on during the week. Counsellors mainly worked Monday to Friday and some patients, if they were good, were allowed to go home as well. There were a few meetings to attend, but Saturdays and Sundays were mainly used for family visits and relaxation. She suggested I go to the morning's relaxation class which was to start at 9.30 prompt. From the way she sounded and looked, I thought she'd just come from it. Although our conversation was brief, I'd gleaned enough to be going on with.

The room was gradually filling up as the odd person in designer tracksuit and trainers wandered in. It was then that my arm was grabbed by someone not much younger than the lady I'd just been chatting to. She was short with grey hair and had a strong German accent. She had a pleasing smile and I thought she was a patient. I looked frantically for a badge. The way I was ogling her chest and the rest of her person, she must have thought I was some sort of pervert. She asked me a little about how I was feeling, how I'd slept and she too recommended the relaxation class, which she said would help with any anxieties I might be feeling. She wished me well and I watched her leave the room. From the way the other patients acknowledged her on the way out, I knew she had to be a member of staff.

Then my name was called out loudly by a nurse in the doorway and I was ordered to join the other patients in the queue for the cocktail trolley. The queue was much longer than last night's, it was a bit like the queue for a cinema blockbuster. But instead of people chatting about their expectations of the movie, all was focused on what was to be popped today. Tablets were given out like dolly mixtures. They came in all shapes, sizes and colours. It was my turn. I was given three yellow ones and two white. I had the feeling I'd somehow been short changed. Some patients had been given a meal when I'd only had a light snack. Once again I downed the pills and didn't bother to ask what they were or what they would do for me.

I'd been in the clinic for less than twenty-four hours and I was beginning to have some doubts. I wasn't sure how long my treatment was to last. I was pissed when I arrived and I hadn't bothered to ask. I didn't know what they were going to do to me.

I've never been a conformist and here I was following the crowd. Being told to join a queue and take a handful of tablets without question. It wasn't me. I've never wanted to be part of a team or take part in group activities. During my childhood I felt that I could never really let myself go and muck in with the other lads, be one of the gang. Once I was asked to play in a Radio One football match in Wales. The last thing I wanted to do was sit on a coach for four hours singing football songs and talking about the size of women's breasts. I played the game, but I refused a joint bath with all the other blokes after the match and showered quietly on my own. Now I found myself, without paying any subs, part of a club.

I stayed in the reception area so as not to miss my relaxation class. It was to take place in the oblong conference room which last night had doubled as the exciting ping pong room. The ping pong table had been pushed aside and exercise mats were strewn across the floor. They were rather small mats, not much longer than a good sized hand towel. Plenty of bum exercises, I thought, after all you can't do much else on them.

Class started promptly at 9.30 with an apology. A young girl was to take the relaxation class, as unfortunately the physiotherapist who usually took it hadn't turned up. I wasn't too perturbed, it was only my first day and our teacher for the day was an attractive girl with fair hair, nice features and quite a lovely bod. There were no complaints from the other male patients either, but there was the odd if-looks-could-kill glare from some of the female residents. The room was busy. A popular class, I thought. We started off with a few general stretching exercises. She told us to reach out, stretch to the side and grab our ankles, all of which we did without complaint.

After the pills I'd popped I felt as though I could do anything with my body, I'd become a Cindy doll which some bored little child had got hold of by the legs and was twisting them well over my head. All I could think was, Don't mess up my hair. It wasn't exactly a Jane Fonda work out, nor were any of the slow rhythmic moves we were given performed with any style or finesse. I looked round at the rest of the health fanatics and it was obvious from our tutor's polite smiles and gentle instruction that she was content that none of the regulars had decided to walk out.

The end of the class, she told us, was normally performed live. Ten minutes of soothing hypnotic chat to enable us to relax. Sadly, our tutor, having been asked to step in at a moment's notice, hadn't been given a script nor had any relaxing repartee prepared. It was left up to a ghetto blaster and a cassette tape. I was pissing myself. The sound of the English countryside filled the room as a Katie Boyle soundalike relayed to the group how the seasons of the year change gently from one to the other and how the setting sun makes one think of a life in the tropics. I was there, on that beach, lapping up those waves. I was totally out of it. I couldn't believe it was the exacting class or the tape that were sending me into a land of slumber, it was those bloody tablets. At this rate I was going to end up with a multiple addiction. I'd come out of the clinic addicted to drink, drugs and willing to do anything to get hold of one of those soothing tapes.

After the class there was only time for a mouthful of coffee from the vending machine when I was ushered upstairs with a handful of others for a meeting of sorts in what was called the Blue Room. I was feeling groggy and stumbled on one or two of the steps. I was given a helping hand by a young lady called Suzanne. Although feeling pretty dire and desperate to get back to my bedroom, I was determined not to give in. I managed to make it up the stairs where I used my time with Suzanne to find out what was to happen next.

She informed me that every morning at Chesterton Grange the patients who are chemically dependent gather in the Blue Room to express their feelings. It's a way of getting to know one another and to understand each other's problems. During the rest of the week, time at the clinic is spent having lectures about one's particular illness and open discussions which can range from a patient recounting his life story to the rest of the class to a member of AA extolling the virtues of life without drink.

Suzanne made me feel at ease. She too was an alcoholic. She'd been at the clinic for two weeks or more. She was very thin with spiky dyed hair. Her late eighties clothes didn't quite suit the surroundings at Chesterton.

We gathered in a large, semi-panelled room, painted white, with a blue carpet and chairs. A large easel caught my eye and I studied the diagrams and graphs scribbled on it. I tried to think of a gag for some of the doodles that had been drawn. Although I was feeling totally out of my tree, the showbiz mind whirred into gear as I desperately tried to think of a one-liner, as if I were on *Win, Lose or Draw*. There were about half a dozen people in the room who positioned their chairs in a circle. I came out with the gag, 'Let's join hands and contact the dead', which went down quite well with Suzanne, but like a ton of sick with the rest of the group.

Judging by people's attire there was a whole cross-section of humanity here. One lady was dripping with gold bangles, necklaces and rings. She was very well dressed, which suited her glowing tan and golden blonde hair. Next to her sat a gentleman I guessed was in his mid forties, wearing a Pringle sweater. I immediately thought golfer/businessman. The Scots chappie that I'd met the previous night, whose name was Jim, was also in the room along with an Arab looking man who said nothing. For some strange reason the Middle Eastern man was wearing a raincoat. Maybe he'd just come in or was about to go out. He sat there with his hands in his pockets. I smiled politely at him and he glared back.

There was very little talking. I thought everyone else was like me, spaced-out newcomers, unsure of their whereabouts and what was to happen next. The golfer/businessman got up and fumbled through a selection of books on the mantelpiece. He found what he'd been looking for and asked if anyone would like to read from it. It was a small book called *Thought for the Day*. No one exactly leapt at the opportunity to read, although some heads turned in my direction. I wasn't going to bloody read, it was my first day. I had problems focusing on the room, never mind a section of small print. I was the new boy being taught how things worked round here. There were no takers, so, with a sigh, he began to read.

Like my little joke, his reading seemed to fall on deaf ears. Suzanne told me later that he was called Raymond and he'd been at the clinic for just one week. He was a London businessman who still continued to do business while receiving treatment.

He was continually late for group meetings and lectures because of his work. Apparently, last week, he had made the mistake of using the facsimile machine at the clinic and had forgotten that the fax, when received, would have Chesterton Grange Clinic written all over it. Minutes after it was sent, his employer phoned back to ask why he'd received a fax from a clinic. Raymond made the excuse to his employer that he was in a private medical clinic for a minor operation.

It was a short Thought for the Day, a small piece of verse. As it was read, most people looked at the ceiling or smiled politely at their opposites. Maybe some folk had taken in Raymond's recital and were inwardly digesting its contents. The way I was feeling, Claudia Schiffer could have stripped naked in the room and the only thing I'd have been able to raise were my eyebrows.

The silence in the room seemed like an eternity until a lady in her early thirties breezed in. She had long brown hair and a friendly smile. Dressed in jeans and a sweater she introduced herself as Val, one of the counsellors at Chesterton Grange.

Val looked in my direction and she seemed to be aiming her introduction mainly at me. I presumed from this that I was the only newcomer in the room. There was a very long pause then Val explained what she had in store for us. Her tone of voice and mannerisms altered as she spoke. Her bright and breezy opening came down to a gentle, more relaxed pace as she explained, 'This morning's group session is for you to express how you're feeling, either emotionally or physically.' She looked right at me. 'For some of you it may be the first time you've ever had to express your own feelings, so feel free to share as much or as little as you like.' To my trained presenter's eye and ear, I knew she must have used those words a million times, but she did it well and I sat back in my chair eagerly awaiting what would happen next. Once again there was a long pause.

It was as though everyone in the room was composing themselves to listen to a bit of Vivaldi or pay heed to a reading of a sonnet by Masefield. My fellow patients performed well. As they adjusted their positions on the uncomfortable seating, there was coughing and the odd bit of heavy breathing. Val asked Scots Jim how he was feeling today. Jim, without hesitation, told his story. He gave meticulous details of what time he went to bed, how he'd slept, what time he'd got up and who he'd met. Even I got a name check.

I felt rather guilty for being such an awkward bastard last night and for giving him so little of my time. He spoke with ease. From the way he spoke I surmised he was used to talking in depth and honestly about the way he felt.

As Val asked each patient around the circle the same question, it dawned on me that soon it would be my turn. I wasn't in the mood to express my feelings openly. Once again, it crossed my paranoid mind that there could be a journalist present. As the others addressed the group, expressing their feelings and emotions freely, I rehearsed mine in my head, like I do before presenting anything on TV or radio. My turn eventually came. I felt very uncomfortable being put in the position of talking to a bunch of strangers. For the life of me I couldn't think how this was going to stop me drinking. I'd done a bit of this open chat before at drama school and here I was again, pre-planning my every word to manipulate people's perceptions of me. I thought it was best for me to decide over the next few days whether this sort of treatment was going to work for me. In the short term, I'd just keep taking the pills and reserve my other judgements until later.

It was my turn to speak. I was very brief. I told the room that I'd checked in last night, I was feeling pretty groggy and I hoped they wouldn't mind if I just sat back and got used to the way things worked over the weekend. That was it, well rehearsed and quite nicely delivered and I didn't even use a presenter's autocue machine or teleprompt.

The rest of the session was spent listening to Scots Jim prattling on about his childhood, family and marriage. It was all very interesting and he filled in a good half hour of the session but, to be honest, I wanted a fag. Val wound the meeting up and we all traipsed out in no worse shape than we'd been in when we'd gone in.

There was a rush on the staircase as people rummaged through pockets and handbags for fags and a light on the way down to the smoking room. I held on to the banister. I felt like I was going to keel over at any moment. I made it to the smoking room by using the wall to prop me up. I felt a bit like James Caan in the film *Misery*, grabbing hold of bits of furniture and using my surroundings to drag myself round. I slumped onto the sofa next to Suzanne and Jim, where they made me feel better by telling me how confused they felt when they first came in for treatment.

They gave me the run-down on what to expect over the weekend. It wasn't much: some more relaxation and another group chat.

I was slightly annoyed that none of the workforce had taken the time or the trouble to explain this. Maybe Val the counsellor could have spared a moment after our group discussion to tell me how long I would be in treatment and why I was being given drugs. New arrivals are bound to be a little bewildered and I was not impressed by them leaving it to the patients to give me an introductory course.

During the afternoon, patients, family and friends bustled in and out of the smoking room. I was content to sit there and watch. I was feeling pretty sorry for myself and thought the rest of the world was happy getting rid of that drunken sod for a few weeks or maybe months. Must be the same feeling when a troublemaker is sent to prison for a few months. I imagined my family and best mates packing their bags and making holiday arrangements while I was away.

The clock on the wall ticked by like an action replay. Twelve o'clock came and I cheered up. The world hadn't forgotten about me. Maria arrived in the doorway of the smoking room. Maggie was still away and I presumed that Maria had been sent to see how I was getting on. Our conversation was somewhat one-sided as I was having real problems getting my act together, due, I think, to the tablets. Maria laughed at my slurred speech and general behaviour. She must have thought I was more pissed than ever.

It was time for lunch, so Maria stayed for a bite to eat. The dining room was full and a queue had formed into the reception area. A few people in the line had recognised me. After years of being spotted, you get to know the tell tale signs. A little giggle or the odd smile, nod or wink. But today was the I'm-not-going-to-let-on-that-I-know-who-he-is look. It starts with a long stare. Once eye and brain have made the connection and a name has been put to the face, it's the I'm-dying-to-tell-someone-else routine. The head is normally turned away from the celebrity and a few whispers are exchanged. Because this part of the performance has to be whispered, one can usually hear the recipient saying 'Who?' Once again the routine is repeated, this time with the additional words 'Don't look now'. I give them ten seconds. Usually a head is turned first of all to look at the general surroundings (in this case the eyes roam the reception area) and then it is as if they were caught by a fishing line. A quick, sharp look at me and eyes back to the front. A few giggles finish off the recognition process and from then it is the odd glance on the way into the dining room.

The menu looked good, with a choice of starters, main courses and puddings. I refused to eat anything, but Maria had her fill while I just about managed a glass of water. The restaurant was packed and I couldn't wait to get out of there. We moved off the table and I asked one of the nurses whether it would be possible for Maria to take charge of me so we could go for a walk in the garden. Maria was eyed up and down and permission was granted.

Maria, I'm sure, had better things to do than take a stroll with me. It was a bit like a walk round a garden centre as we studied the flora and fauna and the huge pine trees that surrounded the clinic. There were paths and walkways that led off all over the place. There was also a pretty stagnant pond and an area that looked like it had once held a tennis court, but obviously since the onset of the popular ping pong table in the conference room it had become overgrown and in need of much attention.

Fellow patients and visitors roamed the garden as I tried to fill Maria in on what had happened since she'd dropped me off the previous night. I also found out exactly where I was. It certainly wasn't within walking distance of Newbury.

Before Maria left she delivered a few surprises from the boot of her car. The first was my portable colour television and the second my Nintendo computer games system, so I could play *Mario Brothers*. At the time I was a real computer games fan. I'd spend hours plugged into the television with a bottle of booze and a packet of fags chasing animated characters with my joystick round computer-generated worlds. *Mario Brothers* was a particular favourite of mine, not least because it was not that difficult to play when I'd had a few.

Maria sped off down the drive and I was summoned by a nurse to join the after-lunch amphetamine hand-out. Three yellow and two white ones and once again I didn't bother to ask what I was taking. The rest of Saturday was a blur. I stayed in my room most of the time, being checked at regular intervals by the staff. There were no locks on the doors, so staff were allowed to come in and out of one's bedroom as much as they liked. I think they knew how lousy I was feeling, as they left me to sleep, only popping in to give me my medication.

I woke and looked at my watch. It was six o'clock in the morning. I'd slept for a good nine hours or more. I hadn't slept that long for ages. I was feeling dizzy and nauseous, my head hurt, just like I'd been hit with a baseball bat. It took me a while to come round, get used to my surroundings and get a grip on how I was feeling. I reckoned it was the after-effects of the tablets that were making me feel so bloody awful.

I didn't know that the tablets administered to me were helping me cope with withdrawal symptoms. They were to stop the DTs, the delirium tremens, that affect people like myself who have drunk constantly over a long period of time. Once I stopped drinking my whole body thought something was missing – it was so used to having alcohol. Once the drink was taken away, as well as making me prone to bouts of insanity and confusion, it wasn't long before, physically, I would suffer from convulsions, shaking, vomiting and palpitations which in some cases can prove fatal without treatment. The medication I was taking helped to reduce all those symptoms. I was on a detox programme that could last anything up to a couple of weeks.

I sat on the edge of the bed and saw myself in the dressing table mirror. I looked dreadful. My face looked like a kids' inflatable bouncy castle, I had black rings around my bloodshot eyes, my stomach hung over my pyjama bottoms and there were bruise marks on my body. How had I got to be like this?

I thought about leaving, but where could I go? Friends and family were fed up with worrying about me and probably felt more at ease knowing that I was receiving some medical attention for my problem.

I wanted to disappear, vanish, go abroad and start again, but I knew that if I left the clinic it would only be a matter of hours before I had a bottle in my hand. I was now over thirteen stone and I looked terrible.

I remembered the days when I weighed nine and a half stone and worried if I had put on a few pounds. I'd gone to seed, let myself go. I was no longer concerned about the way I looked, the way I acted or what people thought of me, so long as I could have a drink.

I shouldn't have felt sorry for myself, though, as I knew it was all self-inflicted and until now there was sod all I felt I could do about it. I reflected on the past, the good old days when things were going so well for me. The times when I was working flat out. One day I'd be opening a shop, the next I'd be doing a two-hour gig with my band and the following day presenting a live TV or radio show. I didn't need a drink to get me on a high, my work did it for me. I enjoyed working with the public, being recognised on the street. But who wanted me now? The kids didn't have a clue who I was. Occasionally a group of fourteen-year-olds would point and stare a bit, but all I was now was a fading children's television presenter. I lived and got work on the memory of my name. If I was offered a job, it was only because the person booking me hadn't realised I'd been off the TV for so long. They were the ones who usually, before introducing me on stage, asked me what I'd been up to. I'd brush them off with things like, I'm on Sky television at the moment or I've got a new series of programmes about to start that are all very hush, hush. They'd fall for it, an' all. The truth was I hadn't been on television for a good few years.

I was saddened by the fact that very few people turned up for my personal appearances. Quite a lot of people asked who I was. I opened, or rather closed, a shop in Suffolk once. I was like the bloody security guard opening the shop in the early hours of the morning with only a few passers-by taking any notice.

I was a fat, drunken slob. Wouldn't the press just love to get a picture of this one! Compare it with the old days. Me in my heyday when I was presenting *Cheggers Plays Pop* and pictures of me now looking like an exhibit at the zoo. I was feeling very sorry for myself and I started to cry. I'd ended up in a clinic: all that smiling, being nice to people, working hard and now look what had happened.

It didn't take me long to snap out of it, though, as I had a more pressing engagement. This time I just about made it to the bathroom. With a huge heave straight out of *The Exorcist*, I threw up. My head spun only in one direction, that of the loo seat. Damn, the seat was down. My projectile vomit bounced off the seat and splattered all over the bathroom's nice white suite and decor. *Bugger!* The walls looked like they'd been ragged by some professional decorators. It took me an age to wipe the place down.

I heard the bedroom door open. It was one of those bloody nurses checking on me again. I couldn't think of a witty ad lib, so I shouted 'Fuck Off!' loudly. She went away with an apology.

CHAPTER SIX

Sunday was much like Saturday, a bit of pill-popping, a lot of coffee and loads of fags. There had been no relaxation class that morning and I was quite content that I'd missed out on the group meeting in the Blue Room. I thought it best that I make a fresh start on Monday. By then I would probably be feeling better and able to put more effort into getting myself on the road to recovery.

My day of doing nothing was disrupted when I was summoned to a small room at the back of Chesterton Grange to have some sort of consultation with a Professor Alpen. He was a short man in his sixties with grey hair. He wore a suit that must have looked great at the fitting but had sadly slipped down and was hanging off his body like a window-cleaner's shammy. He gestured to a chair and I sat on it while he fumbled through his battered brown leather briefcase and found some notepaper and a pen. I wondered what he wanted and why I was there.

He said he knew that I was a new patient and that he wanted to find out a little more about me. I was in a bad mood. If he wanted to know more about Keith Chegwin, he was going to have to work at it. To my surprise, his opening question was, 'What is your name?' Good start, I thought, you've done your homework mate. 'Chegwin,' I replied. He spelt Chegwin correctly, with some prompting from me, but Keith he spelt wrongly and, quite frankly, I couldn't be bothered to correct him. His follow-up question was a real cracker. 'How long have you been here at the clinic?' I smiled as I replied and waited with bated breath for his next Robin Day question. Of course I realised he had to ask me some pretty basic questions, but from our chat he gleaned precious little and he didn't seem to pay much attention to what I was saying. His ears pricked up, though, when I told him I was in show business. He said he'd treated a lot of stars in the entertainment world and he felt sure he could be of help to me. I was surprised when he gave me the names of some very well known celebrities he'd treated.

Confidentiality, I thought, was certainly not at the top of his list. He worried me. Maybe he'd use my name as a reference when dealing with other showbusiness personalities. Our meeting was very brief, just enough time for him to grab a few details which included my drinking history, family life and a little background information. As I spoke he made notes, occasionally asking for a bit of repetition so he could write everything down in his own sort of shorthand or, as I viewed it, scrawly scribble. We shook hands and he said he'd catch up with me in the week.

I left the room and glanced back to see if he was wearing a name tag. For all I knew, I could have been chatting to one of the cleaners. He wasn't wearing one, so I presumed he must be some sort of bigwig.

As I headed for the smoking room, I thought about a drink. I didn't want to be in this place answering all those bloody stupid questions and mixing with people whose problems were, in my view, much more severe than mine. I felt sure that, given a bit of time, I could quite easily give up on my own.

I found Suzanne in the smoking room. She said that she was surprised to see me so soon and wondered why I'd had such a brief consultation. I was informed that consultations normally lasted a good forty minutes. Mine had been less than fifteen. I know I had not been exactly helpful, but I was not impressed.

Lunch was being served when Maggie phoned to say that she was back home and would bring our daughter over to visit me later that evening for some dinner. Rose was only three at the time and didn't really understand why I was in a clinic. Being a child, she just accepted it. Maggie told her that Daddy was ill and needed a rest and she seemed to be happy with that.

When they arrived, I was so pleased to see them both. Rose brought me a card that she'd drawn herself with 'Get Better Daddy' on it. I still have it. Rose tucked into a little supper and we played in the garden together for some time. I drew on all the energy I could to chase her round the trees and shrubs. By the time she left, I was totally exhausted.

As the car drew away, I cried. I wasn't sure how long it would be before I'd see them both again. The thought of not seeing Rose and Maggie made me panic. I started to shake and sweat again and I felt very on edge. I was having difficulty breathing. I headed back to the safety of the clinic. Orders came once again for me to get my regular dose from the junkies' trolley. I have to admit that I had the feeling those pills were keeping me alive.

Sunday evening turned out to be very busy. Janice my sister came over with her other half Paul. I was delighted to see them both. They took the piss out of me as normal. I told them it was the drugs I'd been given that made me slur my words and stagger, but they reckoned I had a secret supply of booze hidden somewhere in the clinic. I showed them round the place and Paul gave me a game of table tennis. I'm sure he suggested having a game for his own amusement value. Playing ping pong against me is like taking on a revolving clothes horse on a windy day.

Patients started to return to the clinic now from having spent the weekend at home. I found out that if you were a good boy during your stay you were allowed a weekend at home, so that you could accustom yourself to your new life in the outside world without a drink. It was a way of reintroducing yourself gradually into society. Some people, I was told, had abused their break and come back worse for wear. But in the main, most people found it a useful exercise. The counsellors advised that if you felt uncomfortable outside, you should head back to the clinic immediately.

I started talking to a chap who was probably a few years younger than me. Dave was a real Cockney, who'd been in and out of the clinic more times than he could remember. I got on really well with him and enjoyed his company. He wasn't like the other patients. He didn't appear to be embarrassed about being in treatment. I got the feeling that he was a loner, not part of the group system at Chesterton. I chatted to him about the other patients. He told me in no uncertain terms what he thought of most of them, and advised me to steer clear of the 'nutters', his way of saying psychiatric patients. Chesterton Grange catered for all types. Dave's 'nutters' were the patients who were in for manic depression, agoraphobia, bulimia, anorexia and the like.

The psychiatric patients seemed to mix with their own kind as well as have group therapy and lectures together. Dave advised me to keep away from one guy in particular, called James. James had been at the clinic for some time; Dave wasn't quite sure why, but one night he had asked Dave if he fancied a game of cards. One of the rules at the clinic is that you aren't allowed to gamble for money. Dave agreed to play poker and suggested that if he won, the prize would be a bit of nookie with James's girlfriend. To put it in Dave's words, 'James went ape-shit' and threatened to kill him. From then on, Dave feared for his life.

I enjoyed Dave's company. He told me that the first time he was allowed home for the weekend, he never made it. He only got as far as the local pub. He had good intentions, when he left for his vacation, but thought that some liquid refreshment might ease the tension of having to go back to his family home. He opted for the nearest pub rather than the train, and the locals were more than happy to accommodate him. He bought them many a round, but unfortunately, when he was well over the yardarm, he declared to his newfound friends at the bar that he was staying with friends at Chesterton Grange. It was then the landlord called the clinic and Dave's weekend was curtailed.

I'd found a friend at last. He may not be the ideal chap to get sober with, but he was someone I could relate to. Someone of my own class who I could have a laugh and a joke with and make some light in these depressing surroundings.

I'd been at the clinic for less than two days and I knew inside that I wasn't really giving the place a chance. I'd been pretty off-hand with Professor Alpen: I was already slagging the place off. I remembered my chat with the old lady: the weekend was for people to inwardly digest and reflect on the past week. Having not been there the previous week but still left with my thoughts, I was bound to be cynical, critical of this new environment.

Throughout that night I fought with the sheet on my bed. I tossed and I turned. One minute I'd wake up sweating, the next I was freezing. I dreamt of secret drinking in my room.

At seven o'clock the following morning I got out of bed content to have made it through another twenty-four hours without a drink.

It was Monday, the start of the week. The weekend was over and it was time to wipe the slate clean and start afresh.

The first lesson of the day was to take place in the Blue Room at 9.30. I headed for the smoking room and watched it fill up. I presumed that nearly every patient in the clinic smoked as the place was packed. I made conversation with Scots Jim and Suzanne, who told me I was in for a busy time. They said that most people who, like me, were on a detoxification programme, taking tablets to help with the withdrawal symptoms, usually fell asleep during lectures and group therapy, much to the amusement of all the other patients. I have to admit I was already nodding off and could have taken to my bed at any given moment. But I was determined to get a grip and give it my best shot. My optimism kept me going. I felt that it had been a bloody awful weekend, I wanted to put that all behind me and get on with what I hoped was to be a good week.

Suzanne took on the roll of an American air hostess and shunted me round the room, introducing me to a score and more of people without fumbling over one Christian name. Don't you just hate people who can do that?

Then it was time to go upstairs to the Blue Room and off we traipsed like a herd of cattle.

This time, there was no circle of chairs, as our first hour was to be spent having a lecture. There must have been about twenty people in our group and, unlike on Saturday, there was no shortage of readers for the book *Thought for the Day*.

Sadly, the reading was interrupted constantly by people entering the room late for class. Raymond the businessman offered his apologies like a naughty schoolboy, but one guy made a more than noisy entrance. During our restful reading he burst into the room, coughing, spluttering and blowing into a dirty handkerchief. He had an olive complexion and I presumed he was of either Greek or Arab origin. Wearing scruffy, crumpled trousers, like he'd slept in them, and a pair of those open slip-on slippers that seem to proliferate in Marks and Spencer during the summer, he acknowledged everyone on his way in and plonked himself in the only vacant chair in the room. On taking his place, he started to play with his nose. He smiled at me while shifting his finger from one nostril to the other, only giving his nose some relief when he scratched his crotch. I felt sure that if other parts of his anatomy had been accessible he would have had a finger in those. As he struggled to bring up a lump of phlegm and made no apologies for it, I could see other people in the group turn away so as not to catch sight of his open activities.

Our attention was broken when our lecturer arrived. He was dark haired and well dressed, wearing a sports jacket, slacks, shirt and tie. He reminded me of a car salesman. His shirt, I noticed, had splatterings of blood on the collar from shaving. I instantly thought that he'd slept in and was in a rush to get to work. He introduced himself as Gary. He spoke to the group and exuded confidence as he paced to and fro in front of the easel acknowledging patients who had been at the clinic for some time and nodding at newcomers like myself. He paused for thought and to ask whether old members of the group would mind if he repeated a lecture which they'd heard before. No one seemed to object. It confirmed my thoughts about him getting up late.

Gary was quite a showman and his lecture on the effects of alcohol on the body was interspersed with the odd gag. He told the group how he'd seen some newcomers arrive at Chesterton, all set for a holiday; how some arrived with their personal computers and their golf clubs ready for a break from the family and the pressures of work. One time he saw a Volvo race up the gravel drive and an old lady step out. She opened the passenger door and an old man, who was obviously pissed, fell out. She shouted to the staff at the Grange, 'Sort the bastard out', then promptly got back into her car and drove off leaving the poor old bugger behind.

The hour sped by and the lecture held many surprises. Until now, no one had ever given me any medical explanation for not drinking or what was likely to happen if I did. Gary gave me food for thought. Most alcoholics are aware that if we drink again, we find it difficult to stop. He told us that our bodies are like computers. Over the years they learn to retain all the data that's been fed into them. That data is always there and can be recalled at a moment's notice. It's just like when you recognise someone in the street: in less than a millisecond you are able to put a name to the face, where you've seen it before, remember the time of day you saw that person and even what they were wearing at the time. When I stopped drinking alcohol, my drinking threshold was probably about two bottles a day before I conked out. My brain and my body, on my last drinking binge, had stored that information somewhere in its data files. That information stays there on file for the rest of my life and I can't erase it. Whenever it is given the right signals, like 'Have just one drink', it whirs into action and says, 'Hey! Keith's drinking again, I must remember what he likes to drink and how much he can consume. Oh, look. Here's the file, it says he drinks two bottles a day and he doesn't know when to stop.' Gary made it clear to the group why it's so important not to take that first drink. If you do, you'll be back to where you started in a matter of days, hours and sometimes minutes.

The lecture finished and we were told to be back in the Blue Room in half an hour for our next session. I headed back to my bedroom and had a sneaky cigarette out of the window. I was much happier now. I'd enjoyed Gary's lecture and I felt better now that my treatment had really started.

We spent the afternoon asking each other about our individual progress in treatment. I took a back seat on this one. I didn't know anyone and couldn't tell you whether they were better of worse than when they came in. I was also very drowsy, nodding off a few times.

During the rest of the week I learnt a lot about why people like myself are dependent on drink, the effect alcohol has on the body, the reason we do it and how, if we are willing to give it our best shot, we can stop.

Apparently, over the drinking years, I went from *wanting* a drink to *needing* a drink. My body thought it was the norm to have alcohol as part of its system. Just as a car's engine needs its oil, my body and my brain thought it could only function at its best when it had the right ingredients. When I stopped giving my body what it needed, it couldn't function properly, it started to go haywire. That's why I sweated, had fits, palpitations, panic attacks, and felt sick.

Alcohol is also an anaesthetic and, without realising it, because I was so numbed, I had done untold damage to my body. I'd most certainly lost a lot of my brain cells, which would affect my memory for ever. My heart, liver, gallbladder, pancreas, kidneys and even my eyes had been affected. Not to mention my joints, muscles, bones, skin and genitals. We could stop if we really wanted. But for someone like myself, who was so far down the line, it was dangerous to give up on my own without medical supervision. The consequences of going it alone could be fatal and therefore it was always advisable to consult a doctor before any attempt was made to stop drinking.

For nearly twenty-four hours a day, patients like myself talked drink and little else. I attended everything that was going, from relaxation classes in the morning to chatting with members of Alcoholics Anonymous until very late in the evening. I became a total convert, extolling the virtues and benefits of life without a drink to newcomers. I took pride in telling visitors like my sister Janice what drugs I was taking to help wean me off the booze: fifteen milligrams of oxazepam, ten milligrams of temazepam, one hundred milligrams of carbamazepine, some lactulose to help my bowel movements and orovite to put essential vitamins back into my body lost through drinking. At each pill-popping session, I was at the front of the queue. I was loving every minute of my treatment.

Over a week in treatment and I was called to reception to pick up a telephone message. I was to phone home. A *Sun* journalist had somehow found out that Cheggers was in a clinic and he wanted to know why. It hadn't taken him long and soon the rest of the press would come knocking on the clinic's door asking the same question.

I panicked and wondered whether I should return his call. Over the years I'd built up a good relationship with the news hacks. Nearly all the nationals had my home phone number and I always made myself available for comment, to save stories being twisted and made third party by some television press officer.

I thought my best option was to release a press statement saying that I was in a clinic for stress. Keith had been over-doing it. His workload was too much and he'd decided to take a break and get some professional help. As an added bonus, once the press release had been sent to all the nationals, every journalist that phoned to ask for any extra information or a quote, would be called back and I'd speak to them personally. A press release was faxed off to the papers and I spoke to nearly every national newspaper there was. I told them that the business had really got to me and I was exhausted. I'd tried various ways of getting away from it all and none had worked. I said that I'd been on holiday and in health farms, but everywhere I went I was recognised and pestered by the general public. My best chance of getting a good constructive break, away from it all, was in a clinic. Somewhere I could really relax, play golf, swim and take time to read, all in such wonderful surroundings!

Most of the papers ran the story I'd told them, although some were more persistent. The odd photographer was seen lurking in the grounds of the clinic and told to beat it by the staff. One day I was told there were two of my mates in reception, they were passing and had popped in for a coffee. Nice try, guys. I'm not sure which paper they were from, but they were told to leave. It all died down quite quickly, though, and I was allowed to get on with my so-called 'vacation' in peace.

Through group therapy I got to hear a lot about how other people started to drink, how bad their drinking had become and why they had eventually ended up receiving treatment. Their stories weren't too dissimilar to mine.

As well as the group sessions, each patient was allocated a personal counsellor to whom they could open up. There are a lot of things some people wouldn't want to talk to a group about and one way of getting rid of old ideas and things that troubled you, past or present, is to come clean on a one to one basis with someone you can trust. Someone you can talk to without fear of reprisal or reprimand.

Unfortunately, I didn't really take to my counsellor, a nifty looking Irishman called Roger Brown. He was the person Maria had spoken to about my coming in to have treatment.

This was my first ever meeting with a counsellor and I wasn't too sure how I was expected to behave. Roger took me into a room behind the reception desk. He wore a grey suit that was well creased at the elbows; he folded his arms when he sat down. He also crossed his legs, his left leg pointing away from me. I saw a documentary once which said that if a person crosses their legs away from you, they are either not keen to chat to you or they don't really want to listen to what you have to say. Whether that's true or not, he obviously hadn't seen it.

Roger had short dark hair that needed a slight trim and dark eyes that reminded me of a fruit machine. One tug of his ears and three cherries would come up. He wasn't a bad looking bloke and spoke with a soft Irish accent. Occasionally, it was so soft I couldn't hear what he'd said. Now he enquired as to how I was feeling, how I was getting on, and then asked me if there was anything I'd like to talk about. My immediate thoughts went to the toilets just behind reception: they were constantly bunged up and smelt. I wondered whether he could have a word with the maintenance man. My only other enquiry was how long I was to be in treatment for. He told me four weeks was the minimum, but one could generally expect to stay longer. It depended on the individual and how much progress they were making. Our session lasted about thirty minutes during which time I told him about my drink history, my family and my career. I don't think I was boring him, but he eventually looked in his diary and said that we'd meet again soon. He also added that he was on call to answer any questions twenty-four hours a day. I wondered if he'd honestly mind me calling him at two in the morning.

On 5 November, Bonfire Night, there was a fireworks party at the Grange. All the patients and some of the staff gathered outside for an evening of sparklers and merriment. Janice and Paul came to visit and scoff hamburgers as we watched the Chesterton gardener set off fireworks like First World War doodlebugs landing on the Isle of Man! Each detonation seemed to take an age, but we kindly acknowledged his efforts by giving him a few gasps and a roar as each one lit up the grounds of the clinic. The fireworks at least took my attention away from a delegation of doctors who had gathered inside for some sort of conference in the ping pong room. Every so often, I was told, Chesterton invited general practitioners round to explain more about what went on in the place, in the hope that the odd doctor might refer someone from their own surgery for treatment. As we partied with our sparklers and baked potatoes outside, they seemed to be having a whiz of a time inside. But as we sipped our mineral water and non-alcoholic punches, they sloshed back glasses of red and white wine in full view of all the patients through the conference room's large windows. I wondered whether this was one of the clinic's little tests and thought we might be asked questions about it in the morning. One of my alkie mates was already asking a few questions of his own, like 'Where do you think they keep it?' 'Can we sneak a bottle out?' At one point, it looked as if this wasn't so much a gambit for getting more patient referrals as a way of sorting out the doctors themselves who had a problem, as more than a few of them had downed a carafe or two before our complaints were heard and the evening was apparently curtailed.

The following morning, the drinks and firework party was brought up in the group session. I was surprised, like all my fellow patients, that the idea of alcohol being consumed on the premises was swept under the carpet by the counsellor, who used it as an example of what the alcoholic was going to have to face up to in the outside world. Maybe next time they might invite some sex therapists down for a chat.

Occasionally, patients were given the opportunity either to pop down to the local leisure centre for a bit of exercise or stay behind for a lecture on life management. Most hands went up when the offer came to get out of the place for a breather. Old hands at the clinic were in there first, and places had already been taken for snooker and swimming. I found myself lumbered with playing badminton with Suzanne; it was the only way I could get out. I hate sport, but I was determined not to be left behind for a boring afternoon of chit chat. As we boarded the

Chesterton Grange bus en route for the leisure centre we were like a coach party of school kids.

On our arrival, the receptionist behind the desk took a definite step back. She'd heard it was a party from Chesterton who were now about to take over the premises. A careful eye was kept on all patients by our accompanying nursing staff, probably in fear of one of us doing a runner. I forced myself into playing half-hearted badminton with Suzanne, although I have to admit she was a whiz with the racket and shuttlecock. She had very little difficulty winning each match as I played a bit like a fixed wing aircraft.

The next time I was asked to go down to the sports centre, I put my hand up to play snooker. Unfortunately, eight other people had their hands up before me. I was the ninth and I didn't have a partner to play with; however, I persuaded our guardian to let me watch.

At the time, I seemed to have made friends with one of the psychiatric patients, a young guy called Kelvin. He was tall, dark haired and skinny. He very rarely spoke to anyone and never uttered a word during any of the group lectures, open to all patients, whatever their needs. Once in a while, for some unknown reason, he'd just get up and go, walk out of the class and no one would see him for days. As part of my new outlook on life I had made the decision to help others with their plight.

I knocked on Kelvin's bedroom door one day and he let me in for a one-sided chat. I did a lot of talking and from that day onwards he tended to stick with me. If a group formed in reception, he wouldn't talk, but he'd sidle up to me and listen. If there was a chair free next to me in the smoking room, he'd be there. When the hands went up for swimming, to my surprise, his went up, too. As I appeared to be his one and only friend, I thought that to make him feel more secure I'd stick with him on our outing. There was no way our friendship was going to make me wear a pair of trunks and get wet, but I was willing to keep an eye on him for the duration of the expedition.

We arrived for our afternoon's activities and Kelvin went off to get changed whilst others headed off to play squash, badminton and snooker. I watched the swimmers for a short while, but spent most of my time asking for change for the coffee machine. It was weird being out of the clinic. I looked at the aliens from the world outside and every time someone passed me, I'd smell them to see if there was a drinker in our midst. After forty minutes or so, the swimmers left the pool and went to dry off. Shortly after, I heard some rumpus going on in the changing rooms. I heard Kelvin's voice and popped my head round the door. He was standing there naked, wringing out a pair of swimming trunks. Apparently, while he was giving them the odd twist an old bloke had passed him and told him not to do it over the seats. 'People have got to sit there,' he'd said. The old guy had made Kelvin cross. As I tried to calm him down, he threatened to beat the old man up.

At this point, I left the changing rooms to look for some more change so I could buy Kelvin a drink. Then I waited for him to emerge, coffee in hand. Only then did I see a uniformed member of the leisure centre staff walk across the reception area with one of the changing room doors in his arms. It was in much need of repair. Apparently, while I was off looking for some loose change, Kelvin had gone in search of the old guy who had annoyed him. He found a locked changing room door and reckoned the old man was in there. He then proceeded to kick the door off its hinges, but to no avail, as his prey was in the pool doing thirty lengths. Luckily, my other Chesterton buddies had managed to dissuade him from going into the pool fully clothed.

On leaving the leisure centre, I felt like Jack Nicholson in *One Flew Over the Cuckoo's Nest*. I was proud of my little gang. Although we were at fault and one of us had fucked up, we'd stuck together. Kelvin was quiet but the rest of the group had spoken for him and we had all asserted our feelings of kinship towards him. We all had our problems, but we were willing to work them through together. For the first time, I felt I had a chance of making it.

In my fifth week, I exuded confidence and was desperate to leave. The lectures were becoming repetitive, I was bored with the other patients and I was now able to reel off the menu for the next few days and more. However, that confidence was about to be given an extreme blow. A couple of my ex-drinking friends had been allowed out for the weekend. I was envious of their departure, but late on Friday evening a rumour swept through the clinic that neither of them had made it home. One returned later the same evening more than worse for wear; the other was still to be found. They'd been in treatment for more than five weeks and only hours out of its environment they had gone on the razzle. I spent the weekend contemplating my destiny. Would I drink again? No, never. Not me.

CHAPTER SEVEN

On 7 December 1991, I left Chesterton Grange a shadow of my former self, mentally and physically. I'd lost a bit of weight and I looked a darned sight better than when I went in. I'd been given the official go ahead from all the counsellors to leave and I assumed that, by granting their permission, they were quietly confident of my chances of survival in the outside world.

I arrived home to be greeted by my ever faithful dog Hollie. A stone was plonked on my lap when I opened the car door, which was her border collie way of saying, OK, you've been away for a bit and I know you've missed me, so let's get on with it. I threw her stone and looked at the surroundings I'd come back to. Nothing had changed.

Except for one thing. Maria had gone. It had all been too much for her. She had told me during one of her visits to the clinic that her father had offered her a job with his company and that she was considering a move. Maggie and I were reluctant to let her go, but she, like Maggie, had been through a lot and it was unfair to persuade someone so young to stay.

During my time in treatment the national newspapers had never been off the phone, enquiring whether it was possible to have an interview with the new Keith Chegwin when I returned home. Maggie and I thought it best to tackle this one as soon as I got back. A press call was organised for nine o'clock the following morning at the house.

I felt obliged to attend, being the subject for debate and snapshot, but I was in no mood for all that crap. I didn't really feel well enough to cope with the journalists' prying questions, especially as I would have to lie about being in a clinic suffering from stress.

They turned up with notepads and cameras and I prattled on about how wonderful I was feeling and how nice it was to be back home. I had pictures taken on a snow-covered lawn with Billy our pet pig, who actually upstaged me as he looked more attractive than myself. They fell for the story, hook, line and sinker and the following day's papers relayed to the nation how marvellous life was now I'd gotten over a sticky patch.

For the first couple of days at home I was acting like I was still a patient at Chesterton Grange. I'd get up in the morning and, just like when I was in treatment, I'd ask everyone how they were feeling that morning. I think I must have been slightly brainwashed by all the counselling I'd had. I was doing a bit of a Claire Rayner, counselling everyone who walked through the front door. I'd ask Maggie a hundred and one questions about her well being: whether she'd slept well last night and how she was feeling emotionally. It wore off after a few days though, and I settled down. Life got back to some sort of normality.

I had told the staff at the clinic that as part of my recovery plan I would attend local AA meetings. I kept my word and found out through the phone book where and at what times these meetings were to be held and went to a new meeting nearly every night. As time passed, though, I began getting cheesed off hearing about how depressed some ex-drinkers were and how wonderful life was without a drink from the rest of the group. Sometimes there was something really good on the telly and I wanted to stay in, but I felt obliged to attend to keep people happy as I had done for the whole of my life.

I'd agree to do anything to keep the peace as I always found it difficult to handle anything confrontational. I was known for wearing some appalling lurex and glitter jackets on *Cheggers Plays Pop*: blue and silver striped and red with gold braiding. I looked a real divvy. I only agreed to wear them as I didn't have the nerve to say 'no' to the producer and wardrobe mistress on the series. By the way, I still don't like 'em.

I'd been ticked off many a time at the clinic for being a people pleaser. Both counsellors and patients had told me to be more assertive, frank and, if needs be, more outspoken. If necessary, I should stand my ground and argue it out. That's all very well in the comfort of a clinic with a counsellor at hand who has all the answers, but in the outside world it is a different story. I was finding it hard to put what I'd been taught into practice.

Friends, family and colleagues also found it difficult to accept the new, tougher, stronger Mr Chegwin, the new Keith who would sometimes say no. When I stood my ground in arguments I often found that circumstances became heightened. I knew it was all due to me putting my foot down and standing up for myself; it was my fault. I turned many a polite debate into World War Three.

I couldn't keep it up. Within weeks I was beaten and ended up saying 'Yes' to everything, from work to going shopping and mucking out the horses!

I was beginning to feel that my time in the clinic had been wasted. It was like I'd been on a language course and it wouldn't be long before I'd forgotten all I'd been taught. The clinic had dried me out, sorted me out and kicked me out. Maybe I was suffering from what the experts call 'Dry Drunk Syndrome'.

With this, whether you're drinking or not, your behaviour stays the same. Only time and a lot of hard work can help change that. Basically, you are still a drinker but without the drink. All the things that set you off when you hit the bottle are still there. You still get frustrated, angry, pissed off and more.

One way of coping with the pangs of such frustration is to do a simple check on yourself. They call it HALT. You literally halt for a few minutes and evaluate why you are feeling so fed up, on edge or uptight. You evaluate your circumstances and ask yourself whether you are HUNGRY, ANGRY, LONELY or TIRED. If you answer 'yes' to any one of these, then you're supposed to go and do something about it to relieve the anxiety. By addressing these symptoms directly you can help yourself steer clear of drink.

If you feel hungry, they advise you to go and grab a bar of chocolate or a piece of toast. When I felt hungry there was sod all in the house to eat and I didn't think a tub of sunflower margarine would suffice. When I felt angry, nine times out of ten it was because I was speaking to a journalist from the *Sun* whom I couldn't tell to bugger off. When I felt lonely, it was usually about three o'clock in the morning, when there would be all hell to pay if I woke anyone up for a nice little chat. I felt at my most tired at five in the afternoon when all the animals needed feeding. If I was caught napping then, I thought I'd probably be accused of drinking.

Five weeks in a home for the bewildered, with a large hole in my bank balance to prove it, and I was no better off. Slowly but surely, my thoughts started to turn to drink. I began wondering whether the clinic's counselling, lectures and group therapy had really worked. Perhaps they had done a Paul McKenna and secretly given me some deep-rooted hypnosis so that I would steer clear of drink for the rest of my life. I felt terrible and spent many a day and night contemplating my next move.

I started to fantasise about having a small tot of whisky. While watching television I'd play with a glass of mineral water as though it were an expensive brandy. I'd feel its warmth sliding down my throat and deep into my body. I'd imagine how refreshing a pint of lager would be after a long bike ride and how a glass of champagne would help me to relax and enjoy a late movie.

At night, I'd lie awake in bed planning how to go and buy a drink. Eventually, I had it all worked out meticulously in my head. There was a post office cum general store only a few miles away from my house where I could go and wouldn't be spotted. No one that I knew had any reason to go there or even pass by. I rehearsed in my head how I could get something to drink. I'd pop into the post office to buy some stamps, and while I was there I would do a little extra provisional shopping and ask for a bottle just before the items were being tallied up on the till. I'd been through this routine hundreds of times before but, having been in a clinic and the whole nation knowing that I was there for some kind of stress-related treatment, put me off the idea for a few days.

I couldn't afford to take any chances. My main concern was that someone from my evening meetings would spot me walking out of the shop. If I were to drink again, I'd also have to wait until everyone was out of the house for the whole day, so I'd have time to recover from the effects and the smell on my breath. I waited days for the right moment to carry out my plan. I was on tenterhooks waiting for the opportunity to go and hit the post office. I felt like some shotgun thug about to do a raid.

It was a Wednesday when I started up the Land Rover and headed out of the drive. Maggie was away working, the housekeeper had gone home and it was unlikely that anyone would pop round. I'd been left on my own for the very first time. As I drove to the shop I wondered whether I was doing the right thing. I thought about the weeks I'd spent in treatment and the promises I'd made not to drink again. But it wasn't long before I'd put them all aside. Just the one wouldn't hurt, I thought, and I'd organised things so well. I couldn't possibly fail. Anyway, I wanted a drink.

My heart was pounding when I parked the car. I saw a few pensioners chatting outside and panicked slightly. I thought it was

(*above*) Sister Janice
and the first signs of
the 'Cheggers Chuckle'

(*left*) 'Double
Trouble': Jeff and
Keith

(*below*) Aged ten and eager to sing for my
supper

(*above*) I was one of the Merry Men before I had a drink problem. An early role as Robin Hood

(*below*) A character part in *Black Beauty*. The horse's mane looked better than mine (*LWT*)

(*above*) The stars of *Swap Shop*. Noel Edmonds, myself, John Craven and no Mr Blobby (*Daily Express*)

(*left*) It's just a Coke – honest

(*above*) My home in the country, 1984–93. I never did get round to fixing the guttering

(*below left*) Billy the Pig makes himself at home in the breakfast room

(*below right*) One of my personal appearances. There was always a crowd when it was free to get in

(*above*) Daughter Rose, only hours old, has her first press call with Mummy and Daddy (*Evening Standard*)

(*below*) Cheggers sings pop (whether they like it or not)

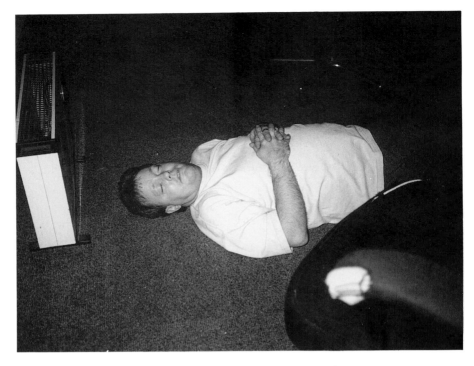

(*above*) A night on the tiles – the carpet or even the drive

(*below left)* Cheggers can't be boozers

(*below right*) Letting the train take the strain

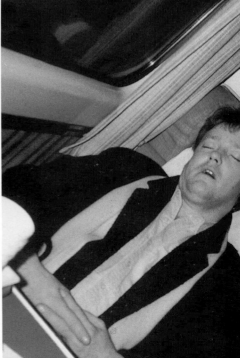

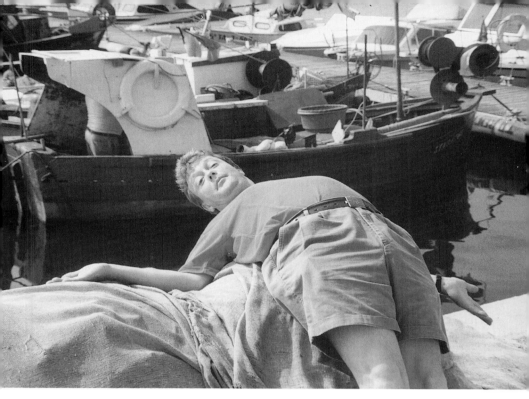

(*above*) A drinking holiday in Spain and my impression of a tequila sunrise

(*below left*) The locals now know my nickname and my age

(*below right*) In panto. 'Oh yes, he is. Oh no, he isn't'

(*above*) Sober in my recording studio where most of my drinking was done

(*below*) My faithful friend Hollie the Collie

a Thursday and the shop was going to be full of old folk queuing for their weekly pensions. I walked in and, as planned, I bought my stamps. I continued through the store and bought a few groceries. I knew exactly what to purchase: half a dozen eggs and some fruit, all of which were bio-degradable so could be chucked out of the car window on the way home. I went to the till and the lady rang up the total. As she was doing it, I casually asked for a half bottle of Bells whisky and she obliged. It went like clockwork. I'd done it! I smiled all the way back to the car.

I waited until I was well away from the shop and into the Berkshire countryside before I unscrewed the top of my bottle. It was like a scene from the film *Groundhog Day*, I'd repeated the same scenario so many times in my head. I held the bottle to my lips and, before I drank from it, I smelt its pleasing aroma. It was wonderful. I took a gulp and felt its warmth slide down the back of my throat and through my chest. Invigorating, friendly, rejuvenating. It felt like it was all happening in slow motion and I savoured every moment of it. It was like an old friend that I'd missed and it was nice to have him back. I rummaged through the dashboard of my car but I couldn't find any strong mints or an old Fisherman's Friend, part of the accoutrements for drinking that I'd forgotten to buy. I bottled out of taking my half-finished treasure home in case someone found it, so on the way back I slowed down past a hedgerow and threw the bottle with accuracy into the undergrowth, somewhere where I knew I could find it later.

For a short time I felt guilty about letting the poor sods down who had trusted me to be on my own. But it wasn't long before that passed. I thought about nothing else but that bottle in the hedgerow for the next few days. I wondered whether someone else might find it. Had I screwed the top on properly and would I find it again? I made an excuse to pop out to the local shop to buy some cigarettes.

On the way, I slowed down past the drop zone. I could see my bottle covered in morning dew. The temptation was too great. That bottle was beckoning me, and I stopped and finished off its contents. The same afternoon my desperation to have another drink was so great I risked disappearing from the house to buy another one. That was it, I was back on the treadmill and would use any excuse to get out of the house. I'd go shopping, walking or cycling to get a drink.

Back to my old tricks, I now had all the extra equipment necessary to complement my activities. Aftershave to disguise the smell of alcohol, a packet of Extra Strong mints for obvious reasons and a bottle of Eye Dew to keep my eyes looking clean and take away any redness. I'd also bought a few bottles of Night Nurse, which I'd hidden in case of dire emergencies. A new trick I'd picked up from the clinic was drinking cough mixture, which contains alcohol. I placed a bottle in the bathroom and secretly guzzled it in the evenings.

I spent Christmas with my in-laws in Leicester. It was one hell of a Christmas. They knew about my drinking and I pretended during my stay with them that I was on the wagon. Little did they know, though, that I was helping myself to their drinks tray at any opportunity. I was always first on my feet to do the pouring: one for them and two for me. I'd also stay up late until everyone had gone to bed so I could pop into the pantry and help myself to swigs from every bottle that was open. Bailey's Irish Cream, brandy, crème de menthe, sherry, and more. Every conceivable cocktail. Some nights I was so pissed I only just made it to bed. Throughout my entire stay I managed to continue my secret drinking with no one any the wiser.

I remember being told by lecturers at the clinic that just one drink is enough to stimulate the whole body into thinking Wow! We're off again. I'd been out of treatment for less than four weeks and I was back to where I started. I was beginning to feel a sense of guilt and remorse for what I'd done. I phoned Roger and he suggested that I come back and stay for another four weeks. I made a promise to him that this time I was going to make a real go of it.

On 27 January 1992 I was back at Chesterton Grange. I didn't let on that I was reluctant to go back, but I had to. Eventually I was caught out; I'd been a naughty boy, and had no option but to return to keep Maggie and my family off my back. I was looking forward to the Egon Ronay menu and comfortable surroundings, but the lectures, group meetings and counselling were about as exciting as a re-run of the TV series *Crossroads*.

I got a taxi on my own to the clinic to save a long journey of being nagged and promising not to fuck this one up. Soon, I found myself back in the reception area being consoled by patients and the odd passing counsellor about my unfortunate relapse. To be honest, I couldn't have given a toss, but my acting was good. I wasn't happy to be back and I had become sceptical of my reception committee.

A nurse went through my bags to make sure I hadn't brought any illicit substances in. I was told to stay in my room as I reeked of alcohol and they didn't want me to mix with the other patients for fear of them all leaving the premises in search of a Peter Domenic's. Roger the counsellor came to my room like Annie in the film *Misery*; he always seemed to have a smile on his face and a look that made me think he'd like to break my ankles. I now know my reaction to him and my surroundings had nothing to do with his counselling or the clinic's treatment, it was me. But I felt I was banged up, like in a prison. I didn't want to be here, but if I had to, they were going to have a fight on their hands. I wasn't exactly responsive to Roger's questioning.

Over the next few weeks it was the same old story. Some drug taking, a bit of the usual group therapy, the same old repetitive lectures which started with 'I know some of you have heard this before, but I think it's well worth repeating again', a few tea breaks in between and the odd game of ping pong with one of the nutters.

I played ball some of the time, but I felt that during my stay this time I wasn't being treated as a priority patient. I'd messed up and because of my relapse I felt left out in the cold. One morning I decided to throw a wobbly, draw a little attention to myself. During one of the sessions I made the group aware that I wasn't happy with the treatment I was receiving. I told them that since my return I hadn't seen a counsellor. I was lying. It wasn't long after my outcry, though, that I got a little more attention from the staff.

I found that speaking up worked wonders, so I started to have some fun during the lectures. I asked one counsellor in front of a group of twenty or more patients what the success rate was at the clinic. I knew that no clinic in the country had an answer for that one, but it was nice to hear him struggle and I found that it left certain members of the group with some doubts as to their own success at the clinic. The following day, I asked another counsellor whether he had a drink problem. 'No' was his reply. I'd got him exactly where I wanted and followed it up by enquiring how he professed to know so much about alcoholics and whether his knowledge had come from a book or from grilling mates in winebars. If the window had been open, I'm sure at this point he'd have leapt through it. He couldn't answer me.

From then on, I made a point of attending every lecture going just to cause a stir. It was a challenge for me to try and push the experts to the limit. I'd question absolutely everything. I was purposely becoming a pain in the arse and, although they never let on, I think they knew it.

Family visits were few. I saw Rose for a few hours at weekends and Maggie used to pop in to say hello. At the time she was also doing some research for a series of articles for the *Today* newspaper about people who were having various types of treatment. I was surprised when she decided to have some counselling sessions of her own with Roger. After three or four, she said she'd found it useful to air her feelings and she appreciated how having someone to talk to could help overcome many a problem. Good constructive counselling helped lots of people in all sorts of ways with their drinking and physical and psychological problems. Even some phobias could be overcome by talking them through.

I'm not sure what sort of counselling Maggie had requested but, only a few weeks into her private sessions with Roger, I was summoned to a joint one with her and was told by our counsellor that our relationship had come to a turning point and that our marriage was at an end.

To this day I couldn't tell you word for word what he said, but I took hold of the irrefutable fact he'd declared our marriage over. I couldn't figure out why he had been the purveyor of such bad news. I was totally confused and cried as he spoke. I'd had little warning as to what to expect at this session.

Maggie had, admittedly, some weeks before said that she thought our marriage was over. Unbeknown to her, I also knew that she'd been speaking to a solicitor. I'd found a couple of dates in her diary and an odd piece of paper with a phone number on. I'd called the number and found it to be a divorce solicitor's office. So I shouldn't have been totally surprised.

But it was Roger who baffled me. I couldn't understand why he'd taken it upon himself to speak on such a delicate matter. Maybe Maggie had decided, quite rightly, that it was better to have someone with authority and strength to relay succinctly a situation that had been on the cards for a long time. That way, the message would have to sink in. Maggie had been through an awful lot and I'm sure if it had been left up to her to furnish me with the news, I, with some careful and clever manipulation, would have reversed the entire situation and made her re-think it. I was good at that.

Later the same day, I was beckoned to a meeting with Roger upstairs in the Blue Room. I was in a bit of a mess and had difficulty stringing two words together, but during this more informal chat he advised me to seek legal advice. He then told me what I already knew, that Maggie had already hired a solicitor to act on her behalf. He thought it wise for me to do likewise.

I spent the evening in the smoking lounge re-running the day's events over and over again. Although extremely upsetting, I'd taken the news on board fairly quickly. However, I still had difficulty understanding why he who had been counselling me for a drink problem had now also become my marriage guidance counsellor. It was tough enough having to talk to someone about my addiction, but here I was faced with a double dilemma of having to express myself on two fronts. Now I would have to work out at each session which problem should take priority. I felt like some contestant on a tacky game show in which Roger would produce two cards from his top pocket, one labelled 'Divorce', the other, 'Drink'. I had to select one, and take a gamble on answering questions correctly. Neither topics were my chosen subject, nor did I have any of the answers.

I continued to have my own counselling sessions with Roger and the odd joint one with Maggie. However, by this stage, I was in such a state that I wasn't willing to talk to anyone. At every meeting I hardly said a word about myself but listened hard and took mental notes of Roger's every utterance. After our sessions, I went to my room and jotted down what had been said so I could read it over and over again and make some sense of my quandary.

During one of our chats, Roger had suggested I move out of my house and find someone to share a place with. A guardian, chaperon, someone who could keep an eye on me and take care of me. He suggested that I share a place with Maria. Although I thought it might be an idea to move out of my home just for a short while, to give Maggie some breathing space, I wasn't prepared to share my space with anyone else at the time.

Days rolled on and my release date was getting closer. I'd had enough of Chesterton Grange. I felt cocooned in an unreal world. Each day was spent ridding society and life of all its anxieties. I had the feeling that every word I uttered during group or private session was analysed, scrutinised and evaluated for hidden connotations.

I felt set upon and singled out by other patients if I stumbled, misheard or vented my feelings with any anger or animosity. I felt I was beginning to lose my identity. I now viewed others in treatment as conformists. I was never ever going to submit to any sort of conformity, it wasn't me. If the boat was going to keel over, I wasn't willing to go down with the masses. I thought that if I was to stay any longer I might end up even worse. I had mixed feelings about sharing a counsellor with my wife and I felt that I could handle my drink and marriage problems far better by myself.

I was concerned that with a separation now looming I would lose my daughter Rose. Having seen how other people's lives turn out through divorce, I was darned sure I wasn't going to make any mistakes. At that time, I thought it best to try and repair our marriage for Rose's sake and for my own personal selfishness. I still couldn't accept Maggie's ultimatum.

When I left Chesterton for the second time, an odd thing happened to me. During one or two of the group therapy sessions I would get a strange pain in my backside. I thought it might have been the chairs they provided as some days us patients spent nearly six hours in them. When I went home I was still troubled and had difficulty going to the loo. I thought about going to the chemist to see if there was anything on the shelf that I could take; I most certainly wasn't going to ask anyone in the shop for assistance. If I'd have told our local pharmacist I wanted something to soothe pains in my arse, he may have blamed it on the profession I was in. I suffered the agony for a few days more.

One Saturday morning I was in so much agony I phoned my local surgery and arranged an appointment. When I arrived at the surgery the doctor didn't appear to be too happy to see me, as he had had to come in specially. It was the same guy I'd phoned to ask for help when I tried to stop drinking the first time round and he'd told me it was all my fault. He slipped on a pair of rubber gloves and I heard the tops of them crack as he asked me to roll over on to my side and show him mine. It was a bit like that television series on the medical profession called *Your Life in Their Hands* but this was a bit more like *His Hands in My Life*. He tackled my uncompromising position like a plumber with his arm down a U-bend trying to extract a donkey. At one point he told me to stop moaning and push my knees up to my chest: the only problem was his hand felt like it was in the way. I joke about it now, but the pain was unbearable. He told me I had a fissure, gave me some pessaries and told me to buy some painkillers if it got worse.

During my visit he also quizzed me on my drink problem and asked if I knew a few people at the local AA meetings. None of the names he gave me did I recognise. I reckoned it must have been some kind of test, and once again I knew this man was of no help to me. During his rubber glove examination, what he'd neglected to see, and heavens knows how it escaped his notice, was an abscess that was now the size of a golf ball. Luckily, some friends of mind offered to run me over to their more observant doctor who examined me and told me to head straight for Princess Margaret's Hospital in Swindon. As soon as I was admitted I was put under general anaesthetic and the abscess was removed. The surgeon's fear was that it would have burst and the toxins would have poisoned the rest of my body.

After the operation I came round very quickly in a small ante room next to the operating theatre. I sat bolt upright and said hello to a couple of the medical staff still in their theatre gowns. They looked somewhat bemused when I enquired how the operation had gone. One of them checked to make sure I was awake, as most patients don't stir so quickly after having been given a general anaesthetic. At Chesterton Grange, I'd been told to make doctors aware of my drink problem as most alcoholics build up a tolerance to anaesthetic, so it has to be adjusted accordingly. No good you waking up halfway through a triple bypass operation and asking for a bit more. However, I'd forgotten to say anything.

I'd always feared going into hospital, but I must admit I enjoyed my stay and was sad to leave. I'd spent nearly a week in hospital and it took a few more before I could move around. They'd dug a hole at the top of my bottom three inches long and about two inches deep. Once I was home, nurses came round every day to dress my wound for me. They weren't from our local surgery but from one further afield. I found out that the doctor at their practice had several alcoholics as patients and was sympathetic to their needs. I made an appointment to go and see him one day and was very impressed at his reaction when I told him that I had a drink problem. Rather than telling me it was all my fault, he was prepared to listen. I told him all about my addiction, how I was still drinking and what I was doing to try and kick the habit. He didn't instantly prescribe drugs or medicines, he just took time to listen and said that if I needed help at any time he was always there.

Throughout all this I was in a dilemma. I'd promised to move out, so it might appear that I was using my latest medical setback as a ruse to stay put. I didn't particularly want to leave my own home, but I thought it may be a good idea in the short term.

Through a discreet local estate agent I was able to find a small two-bedroomed cottage in the middle of nowhere. It was perfect. I could see from a distance any journalist coming to knock on my door. I took my personal computer to sit on a table in front of the main window so if an unsuspecting person peered in while I was out they would think I was using the premises as an office not as a home. For those same reasons I only took a small amount of furniture and clothes. I didn't see the move as permanent and I settled in fairly quickly.

I was living on my own for the first time in eleven years. I had no problem with cooking, ironing and cleaning, but I did have a problem with my own company. I was bored and very lonely. Days drifted one into another. I watched endless television and videos and was at a loss as to what to do with myself. Each morning I'd be woken by bloody pheasants giving their early morning alarm calls. I now know why people shoot them; if they'd only stop breeding them we'd all be happy.

I was also missing Maggie and Rose. They were so close, but yet so far. I made an excuse to phone home and whilst chatting asked if it was possible for me to take Rose to nursery school in the mornings. To my amazement, my request was granted, providing I was vetted before she got into my car. It gave my whole day a purpose and for a short while I was grateful to the pheasants for getting me up well in time to wash and get ready for the school run. In less than a few weeks of living the bachelor life, though, I was desperate to drink again. I bought half a bottle a day and saved my drinking session till the evening; it was my pat on the back for being such a good boy during the day and for abstaining for such a long, long time. Once again, I thought I had control over my drinking.

I continued to go back to the clinic for the odd counselling session with Roger, sometimes with Maggie in attendance. But I'd lost faith in Roger ever since he'd become embroiled in sorting out my marital problems. I felt he could no longer be impartial and objective, as it seemed to me a counsellor should be. I continued to see him, however, more for lack of an alternative than any other reason.

Back in my little cottage, I lived in fear of someone knocking on the door or peeking through the window and catching me with a bottle, so I continued to hide my drink. One day I would conceal it at the bottom of the rubbish bin outside, the next I'd hide it amongst some clothes in the washing machine. I even used a Stanley knife to peel back the underside of my double bed and hide it inside the bed springs.

I invited my mum and dad to see my new pad. I must have been drunk. It was the last thing I wanted, as I would have to control my drinking during their visit. In desperation, I phoned my new doctor. I'd heard about a drug called Emin Everin. I'd remembered the name, as I thought it sounded like Kenny Everitt! It is supposed to help settle your nerves, calm you down and help you to sleep. One of my colleagues in the clinic described it as booze in a pill. I thought that if I could get hold of some, it would at least get me through the weekend.

My doctor was somewhat reluctant to prescribe anything at all, but after some careful negotiation and the promise to only use the pills to help me sleep I managed to get a small prescription which I could collect at my local chemist. Just enough to last the weekend.

My clinic inmate friend was right, it was booze without the bottle. As soon as I got home from the drug store I downed two to try them out. Wow! What had I been missing? The pills don't give you any kind of buzz or high, you don't feel like running against Kriss Akabusi, it just gives you a nice little tickle. I felt relaxed, smooth and life was OK. I took the pills as prescribed when I felt tense, nervous or anxious and I made it through the weekend without the aid of one of my hidden bottles.

It was great having my mum and dad with me. They were good company. It reminded me of the days when my brother Jeff and I shared a flat in London and they would come down from Liverpool to visit us. Mum spent most of the weekend with a hoover in one hand and an iron in the other, while Dad pottered round the garden checking on the local plant and wildlife and suggesting if I was ever to buy the property, how it could be extended.

When they were gone I was another person, the shutters came down and I went off into my solitary world where a drink was top of the list and nothing else mattered.

I'd decided at the time that I wanted to write a book. I hadn't even thought what I should write about, but a novel, I was sure, would come out of thin air as soon as I had the right equipment for the job. I had no use for pen and paper, so I flicked through the local papers looking for an affordable computer. No luck, so I phoned a lot of mates who ran businesses to see if they had any spare ones knocking around. Eventually, my obsession to get hold of one was so great I phoned Maria.

Maria had kept in touch with Maggie, but it was a long time since we'd spoken and I wasn't so sure she was pleased to take my call. I waffled on about how well I was doing and gave her the usual rubbish, congratulating her on her success in her new life as a secretary. I think she was shocked when, out of the blue, I threw in the question, 'Do you have a computer you're not using that I could have?' The point of the phone call became clear and she knew why I was really calling. She cut short our conversation; however, she said that she knew where I was living and she might pop over for a coffee the following Saturday afternoon.

By Saturday, I'd totally forgotten that Maria was coming. By ten o'clock in the morning I'd already done the rounds of off licences and was well into my second bottle by the time she knocked on the front door. I just about remember opening it and asking if she'd like to put the kettle on. The next thing I knew I was waking up at her mum's house in one of their beds.

As I sipped coffee with Maria and her family, she told me that after I answered the front door, I had keeled over in my living room and blacked out. All her efforts to wake me had been useless. Maria at the time had thought it was a one-off: I'd had a drink because I was worried and nervous about her coming to see me. She had reluctantly thought it was best to conceal the bottles I'd drunk and remove my body to somewhere safe in case anyone else popped round to see me. With all the troubles I'd had, she'd decided to keep quiet about the whole thing and get me round to her mum's house to sober up.

It was no easy challenge getting a 14-stone drunken carcass out of the house and into a small car. She tried to lift me and couldn't. She tried to wake me, but still no luck. Eventually, she grabbed hold of both my feet and dragged me out through the back door and on to the driveway. As she hauled my body across the gravel, a car was passing; all its occupants could see Maria was holding the legs of a man who looked like he was dead. Maria couldn't get me in the car quick enough as she was sure that my next visitors were bound to be the Old Bill.

It wasn't long before rumours started locally. Why was Keith Chegwin living alone in the middle of nowhere? I must have been spotted, as the local paper ran a story claiming that I'd found new premises to work in. They even had the gall to show a picture of my country retreat on the front page. Looking back, I can't believe that anyone really fell for the story; they must have known there was something dreadfully amiss as there were such weird goings on. The following day, I was summoned home. Not to move in on a permanent basis, but just for a week to look after the house while Maggie, Rose and a nanny and her two kids took a well-deserved holiday in Spain.

After they'd gone, I was like a steam train that was slowly pulling out of a railway station and gathering speed. My drinking started to increase and with it my anger at them for taking a bloody holiday without me. I was so pissed off that while they were away I decided to relinquish my caretaking responsibilities and check myself in to a health farm.

I made a phone call to a health hydro which was no more than four miles away from the house. Only the really expensive rooms were available so, without considering whether I could afford it or not, I packed and presented myself in the reception area within a matter of hours. On my arrival, I got chatting to a very friendly chappie in the car park. He filled me in on what was going on at the place and also told me that drinking and smoking were not encouraged. However, he said that if I got stuck and wanted to buy some fags or a couple of miniatures, to give him a shout and he'd sort me out with something. I didn't tell him that I'd already brought my own supply of booze and four hundred fags in case of an emergency.

I was given a medical shortly after checking into my room and was told that because of my size and shape the light diet room was the place for me to eat. I was very quick to inform my examiner that I came to the health farm for a break from life not from living.

I spent most of my stay in my room. Each day I was left a card with a whole list of times for the various healthy treatments I could have: keep fit, pool exercises, massage, aromatherapy, peat baths and more. I think during my stay I might have had one massage, but most of the time was spent sneaking in and out of the place with endless bottles of booze. Occasionally, I'd sit by the pool to convince the staff I was there just for a holiday and sometimes I'd apologise to them for missing my treatments, making the excuse I'd been out for a brisk walk.

I was only there for four days as I had to leave for a gig in Torquay at the weekend. It was a performance not to be missed. I was working for a holiday company at the time who booked me to entertain their guests for a whole weekend. Lucky them. Friday evening I would do my own hour's worth of cabaret, with games and competitions for young and old alike. On Saturday afternoon, I'd host a pop quiz followed by an evening's worth of introducing acts in Keith Chegwin's Cabaret Evening. Sunday entailed me acting as referee for the all-in wrestling. The happy holidaymakers' weekend would only finish with my tracksuit bottoms being pulled down round my ankles, leaving the audience asking for more.

There wasn't much work coming in, the money was good, so I was forced to take it. I'd always promised myself that when times were hard I'd do anything to make a living. To be honest, I'd have preferred to be doing something else but I'd passed my sell-by date. The adults knew who I was, but the kids hadn't a clue. I could hear them whispering before I went on stage, asking the holiday reps who was coming on. I had to change the opening of my act to incorporate throwing out goodies, t-shirts and sweets into the auditorium: it created a crowd at the front that I could play to and gave my employers the impression I was more popular than ever.

This particular weekend, little did anyone know it, but the audience were about to get a bit more than they'd bargained for. Unfortunately, due to polishing off the entire contents of my mini bar at the hotel, I can't personally remember the events that took place over the first two days. However, I do remember my chat with the camp's entertainments manager on the Sunday morning, only hours before I was due to pop down and take part in the all-in wrestling. He told me I arrived on Friday evening a little worse for wear and that he'd expected me to do an hour of comedy, music, games and competitions on stage. He and the audience were somewhat surprised that my entire performance lasted only fifteen minutes, most of which was taken up with me chatting to the holiday reps who were there to assist me with handing out the odd prize. Luckily, he was prepared to let it go and made my excuses, telling the holidaymakers I was ill. Saturday evening was no better, however. I must have been on to my second or third round of mini bars by now as I arrived totally blotto. I was introduced on stage, but before I got as far as the footlights, I fell into the drum kit. The audience thought it was part of my routine. It was only when I started to speak that they realised this was no act. I slurred my every word and proceeded to introduce a vent act as Ward Allen and Roger the Wog instead of Ward Allen and Roger the Dog.

I was in blackout and can't even remember being allowed to sleep it off in a back room at the venue. The next thing I recall was waking up the following morning on the bed in my hotel room still dressed in my dinner suit. It was only when I phoned the entertainments manager to ask what time he wanted me for the wrestling and he replied, 'I don't think we want you at all' that I knew I'd really cocked it up this time.

Phone calls flew between my agent and my employers. My agent told them I was going through a bad patch and he would quite understand if they were to cancel my contract for the rest of the summer. Heaven knows why, but they kept me on. I couldn't believe I'd been given another chance. The company that booked me were prepared to let it go just this once and accept that I would never do it again. To this day, I'm indebted to them.

I stayed in my hotel bedroom, too frightened to go home. I was waiting for the phone call from one of the newspapers about my antics and I prepared myself for the ensuing onslaught from the media. How was I going to pass this one off? How could I possibly explain my outrageous behaviour? Someone was bound to call them, as there had been hundreds of people to witness my embarrassing performance. The press would love it, it was such a good story and would confirm their suspicions about the real reason for me receiving treatment in a clinic. But no one from the audience or the holiday company said a word and the whole event seemed to pass unnoticed.

I stayed an extra couple of days at the hotel. I didn't make any plans to sober up and continued to drink myself into oblivion all day. I was my usual self, shaking, sweating and vomiting endlessly. I'd sit on the loo with a glass in my hand for what seemed like an eternity, but time was not on my side. I had to get out of the hotel soon, as my family were about to return from their holiday.

I ordered a cab home and took more than half a day to sober up. I was just sober enough to greet them on their return.

By this time my entire outlook on drinking had changed. It was different from when I had originally wanted to stop. Way back in December I wanted to give up because I'd had enough and everyone encouraged me to do so. But now I'd forgotten all those original ideals and at this point I couldn't have cared less. It seemed that I was far past the point of no return and drink was more important to me than anything. I was prepared to end it all, I'd had enough. I was only happy when I was drinking. These games I played were futile. I was playing them for other people; they were of no benefit to me in any way, shape or form. Whenever I bothered to think about stopping, I would say to myself that I was only trying to give up drink to satisfy other people's needs, not my own. Why did I have to stop drinking? At the time, I honestly couldn't think of a good enough reason. I was going to take control of my own life for a change, and I wanted to continue.

Without considering the consequences, I was prepared to let it all go. I was willing to lose everything – my wife, my daughter and my home – for a drink.

My mum and dad came down to see me again and, once more, I told them I hadn't had a drink for over two weeks. It was the same old garbage as before, but this time I was making up the rules and they were having to play my game. One minute I'd be chatting to them in the kitchen and the next I'd make an excuse to go to the loo to gulp down as much as I could of the whisky I had hidden in a jacket pocket. My mum even had the nerve to accuse me of smelling of drink. I told her, in no uncertain terms, she was wrong. How could I have possibly had a drink when I hadn't been out of their sight for more than a few minutes? Now I realised that not even my mum and dad believed me any more. I just wanted them all to bugger off and leave me alone to get on with my life.

At the same time, Maggie, like Roger, advised me to contact a solicitor as it would be in my best interests to acquire some legal advice and backing. I thumbed through the Yellow Pages and made an appointment to go and see one locally the following day.

I wasn't at all prepared for our meeting. My only concern was how much all this was going to cost and whether it was worth all the hassle. I was sure things would get back to normal within the next few weeks. The solicitor asked me all sorts of questions. I was there for well over an hour and found myself opening up more and more to her prying, but well constructed line of questioning. I told her that for the time being I'd moved out of the house and found alternative accommodation. She told me to move back into my own home straight away. She made it clear that my only crime was getting drunk. I hadn't been sleeping with someone else, I hadn't left the family home. If Maggie wanted a divorce it was her job to go and do it. My whole world had turned around. I came out of the office a new man and thought that, if the worst comes to worst, I had found the right person to handle the job. I didn't know it at the time, but I believe that my fingers had done the walking into the offices of one of the best divorce solicitors in the country. I took her advice and stayed put in my own home rather than in rented digs down the road.

By this time, paranoia had truly set in. I spent most of the time in my recording studio working on some music for a television series called *Keynotes*. As usual, there was a deadline: I had to write 200 tracks within three months. As I worked, I wondered whether the people that came to and from the house were talking about me. I was desperate to find out what they were saying.

I bought an intercom system and spent a few days taking the whole set apart and rewiring it with a few little additions of my own. When the coast was clear, I used the telephone wires that ran from the studio to the house to wire up all areas in our home so I could hear what was going on from the comfort of my studio armchair. I ran cables under carpets, along windowsills and even incorporated my daughter's baby alarm as part of the listening device. I tested the system to make sure all was working and had a switch on the master machine so I could tune into each room individually and listen. I could also hear what was going on over the telephones and I even installed a security camera, with microphone attached, so I could see and hear anyone outside the house or in the garden. It all worked perfectly and no one was any the wiser.

It was a new era of insanity for me. I became an MI5 secret agent who'd listen and record other people's conversations. I was so sick I had a tape machine strapped to my body that was voice-activated; a simple cough would wind it into the record mode.

Sometimes, I'd use the video camera which was permanently set on the breakfast room table to record three hours of conversation while I was out of the house. I'd also use the video to record pictures from my security camera. If I'd been away from home, I'd come back, look and listen to the tapes to find out what had been said and whose car had been parked in my driveway. Each cassette and video tape would be logged, dated and stored.

I heard lots of stories, but the one that saddened me the most – and the one I'd been expecting for some time – was Maggie chatting about moving out to a veterinary friend in the sitting room one night. I wasn't quite sure where she was off to, but by all accounts her move was imminent and she wasn't going to let me be one of the guests at her new housewarming party. Within days, Maggie and Rose had gone and I pined for their return.

Most people by this time had started to steer clear of me. I couldn't blame them. I wasn't really much company as the only times I was awake was when I had a bottle in my hand. My dog Hollie was always there, though. Many's the time I'd wake with her straddled across my chest or with her nose under my armpit. She's an odd dog, she never craves affection, but she does enjoy attention. She reminded me of myself at the time: a bit of a loner. Sometimes she'd go missing. I'd search for her endlessly and on my return find her back at the house. For some unknown reason, that dog stuck with me through thick and thin. Normally she wouldn't bother barking, but sometimes, if I was out cold, I would wake to her noises as though she was trying to warn me to get up and sober up as someone was coming. She was always right. When I was drinking in the studio she was always around. She'd lay downstairs or under my mixing desk for hours. In return, I'd chuck a lot of stones for her to retrieve and encourage her to find rats or even spray the hose at her for a while. It was an odd relationship, but it seemed to be the only one I had left that worked.

When Maggie and Rose went, that was it, I was all at sea. A friend of mine came to help record the rest of the tracks for the *Keynotes* series. He'd arrive in the morning and we'd start work, but by midday he'd have to stop as I'd keel over my mixing desk and was out for the count. I don't think he was aware of my drink problem at first. He couldn't fathom out why I'd be the life and soul of the party one minute and the next I was acting like a muppet. I put that man through some rough times. I kept cancelling our studio sessions so as I could get jolly pissed and not have to worry about him coming over.

My other problem was a builder friend who'd pop in to see how things were going. He was more of a hassle as he always turned up unannounced. Nine times out of ten he'd catch me in the act of administering my medication. Sometimes he arrived too late and had to suffer the consequences, putting me to bed when I hadn't quite made it out of the shower or I decided to stay put on the kitchen floor, sofa or curled up on the lawn. Some nights, he'd take me home with him and he and his wife would allow me to sleep it off on their put-you-up. Of course, on leaving their home the following morning, I'd promise never to do it again, but within hours I'd found a bottle and I was back to square one.

I'd cancel business appointments left, right and centre and only when I was sure I could control my drinking for a short time would I remake them in the hope I could abstain long enough to get some work done.

Deadlines came and went, but it was becoming virtually impossible for me to do anything. I was asked to compile a music tape for a local shopping centre – a very simple one-hour tape with jingles and well-known tracks people could hum to while doing a bit of shopping. In the real world, it shouldn't have taken more than a week to put everything together, but ask an alcoholic who's still drinking and you'd be lucky to get anything back in a month. Once again, I had to hire someone else to finish the job. It ended up costing me rather than the client to produce those tapes.

I had an odd phone call one day from some people from Alcoholics Anonymous. They phoned up to ask me how I was. I lied, of course, telling them that all was well and I hadn't had a drink for some time. When I put the phone down, I felt guilty. It was different lying to fellow alcoholics and I was sure they knew that I was telling fibs.

A couple of days later, I found myself going to a meeting. I stopped drinking beforehand, but on the way I stocked up the car in case I felt the need to let rip after putting in my appearance. I listened to people in the room telling the rest of us how they felt and what they were going through. We were all in the same boat. A bunch of drunks trying to get better. There was a lot of hope and help, if I needed it, in that room, but I wasn't yet prepared to go the whole hog. You have a choice when you go to an AA meeting: to speak or just to listen. There's no pressure on you to do anything at all, if you don't want to. You just have to have the desire and the will to stop drinking. It works for a lot of people who are willing to give it a go. But I wasn't ready yet.

I was asked to go and promote my forthcoming Christmas pantomime by appearing in a summer carnival. It was to be my second appearance in Aldershot and I was grateful for the booking as at least there would be some revenue to look forward to at the end of the year. When I arrived I had some trouble in remembering what panto I had agreed to be in. It was *Cinderella* and I was to play the part of Buttons. The promoters for the panto had excelled themselves in making a pumpkin-shaped stage coach that I could walk next to, collecting money for charity. I was two sheets to the wind as I wended my way down the merry back streets of the town. One young chap in the crowd took one look at me and accused me of being 'pissed'. This was not the sort of barracking I was used to and I was determined not to let him or other people go home with the impression I was drunk. He wished he'd never opened his mouth as I lay into him with endless one-liner cabaret gags, much to the amusement of the people around him. The local newspaper published a photo of me falling over and losing the money in my charity bucket. Thank God it wasn't one of those scratch and smell pictures.

I made it to some gigs and didn't turn up to others. My guardian had become my building mate and he spent many a day and night trying to keep me off the sauce. Eventually, I'd had enough of his caring ways and told him to get lost. I accused him of helping me to drink. I told him that if he was there all the time there was no way I was going to get better. I was being very unfair but I had to be left alone and tackle this illness head on. I felt sorry for him as he fell for my story, but he did what I wanted and disappeared.

Now I was free once again to do what I felt I did best. I made up little rhymes as I drank in the morning: a swig at four and no more, a drink at five I'm alive, a drink at six is a fix, a drink at seven is heaven, a drink at eight is late and a bottle before nine is fine. I was losing it and I didn't want to step out of the house for fear of being seen or having to talk to anyone.

I opened up an account at a local courier company. One time I remember ringing to ask them to buy me some drink from the off licence for me as my car had broken down and I had some people coming over for a party. What lies!

Each morning I'd usually wake up about five or six and start my endless drinkathon. By noon, if Lady Luck was with me, I'd lock all the doors and windows, hit the button on the answerphone and keel over for the rest of the day. Sometimes I'd rouse before midnight and occasionally return the odd call to family members to save them coming over. I'd tell them I'd been out all day working or I'd gone to an AA meeting.

I was in hiding one hundred per cent of the time. I didn't want to speak to or see anyone; I didn't want to go anywhere. Day in, day out, I went about my business of drinking. The only people I spoke to were the local shopkeepers or my friends at various off licences. The half bottles I used to purchase changed to full ones and I hardly ate a thing. I lost sense of all time. Days and weeks drifted from one to another and I was never absolutely sure how much I was drinking. Sometimes I would make an effort and only drink a bottle a day, but on most occasions I'd drink till I blacked out and only woke to throw up. There were times when I wanted to die and just end it all. I'd had enough.

CHAPTER EIGHT

Once in a while, the odd press person would come up the drive and enquire about my welfare. Newspaper deadlines for the lighter stories are normally before noon the day before publication. Luckily, I was capable of conversation any time before midday, so it suited me down to the ground if someone came round for a chat. I might have smelt like I'd had a drink and slur the odd word, but from a distance I was capable of holding short bursts of conversation on any subject. Just to be on the safe side, though, I'd speak to my visitors though a window, so they couldn't get too close.

By this time, I knew where Maggie and Rose were living. I was occasionally invited round to see Rose and every so often I would ask when they were both likely to return. Maggie had obviously had enough by now, though. The eternal problem of living life in the public eye never went away. Every day the phone rang and it would be some journalist asking for a quote, or questioning the state of our relationship. She thought it would be a good idea to hold a press conference to announce our separation and get it all over and done with. Sooner or later, the story would come out that we were living apart and she thought it best they heard the story first hand to avoid further harassment.

Maggie would inform the media, but I was required to be at her place at nine o'clock one Friday morning in my best togs.

It was about eight o'clock that Friday morning that the driveway of Lime Tree Cottage started to fill up with eager newshounds and their cars. My dad was staying with me at the time, so I sent him out to redirect traffic over to Maggie's new place.

By the time I got there at nine, I had to struggle past the waiting crowd. Photographers and reporters filled her drive, there was even a local Meridian Television crew. I was in no mood for this sort of attention, so Maggie promised to take charge of the entire session. She told them that we had both agreed an amicable separation, that things weren't working out and who knows what the future might hold. She said that there was no one else involved and at this point in time we hadn't even thought about speaking to any solicitors.

I kept quiet and was surprised when a gentleman of the press informed me that it was exactly ten years to the day that we'd got married. It was 4 September 1992, our anniversary. Ten years ago we'd exchanged rings. I looked across towards Maggie's left hand and saw she'd taken hers off. I quietly asked her why. There was no reply.

After the press call, which lasted all of twenty minutes, Maggie and I went into town and had lunch with Rose. Maggie told me how well I'd done and I, of course, refused to take credit for what had just gone on. I hadn't done a thing. I'd just turned up like one of the invited guests.

Needless to say, we went our separate ways again. I was getting bogged down with work and I felt like going back to a clinic, or the like, just for a break.

One morning I was woken up by the phone. I took a few deep breaths before answering it, so as to give the impression I'd been up for hours. It was a mate of mine to whom I'd promised for the second time that I'd turn up for a photo session. Now I was late due to yet another heavy night. I'd let this chap down so many times. He was a good friend, but there's only so many favours you can ask a mate, so I told him the truth. That I'd got drunk and there was no way I'd be able to make it. He was least impressed but being a close friend said he'd cover for me again. I'd had it up to here, I just wanted to get away from it all.

There was only one person I could honestly talk to at the time and that was my sister Janice. She suggested that it was time I took a real break, not in a clinic, but have a holiday. Later that morning she'd organised a cheap trip for me to Spain through a local travel agent. Janice feared for my life. She thought, if I was to go to Spain on my own there was no guarantee that I'd ever come back. She was right, I couldn't trust myself to go away on my own and not drink. Janice couldn't be my guardian, so I got in touch with Maria. I hadn't spoken to Maria for a long time and she was definitely shocked when I asked her to go away on holiday with me.

Her one concern was that if the press found out about my trip out to Spain with another woman it would start rumours that something was going on between us. It was time to throw caution to the wind. There was nothing going on between Maria and I, so let them write what they wanted. Before we left, I made Maria aware that journalists are posted at every airport. They check all ingoing and outgoing flights for celebrities and the odd president coming through. I assured Maria that I was one hundred per cent sure someone would be there to take our picture. But who cares? As with drinking, people can accuse you of many things, but they can't harm you when you know the truth.

Every package holidaymaker I met on the way out to Spain had their own thoughts about who Keith Chegwin was leaving the country with. I signed loads of autographs on the way out but not one photographer was there to capture the moment. I made up for it with my own camera as I snapped away in the departure lounge and even got a fellow traveller to take one of Maria and I together.

I enjoyed my break. I did some sunbathing, a bit of horseriding and I ate myself silly. I must have been exhausted as I slept for most of the holiday.

Only once did I have a sneaky drink. It was very hot on the beach, so I went off to buy some refreshment. The seaside bar was well away from the sea, sand and sunloungers; it was also out of Maria's sight. I ordered two cokes, a lager and a large vodka. I didn't even drink vodka, but I noticed that the chap who was ordering before me had no problem in getting one from the Spanish barman. I've learnt through experience that if you ask for a whisky, or some drink they've never heard of when you're abroad, they keep asking you to repeat your order. Because of lack of communication the conversation tends to get louder. I couldn't take the chance of Maria hearing the word whisky blurted all over the place, so I went for a guaranteed, no questions asked kind of drink. I'd gulped down the vodka and the lager before I'd even been given the change, then I sauntered off down the beach and back to my sunlounger for a kip. Maria was none the wiser.

On our return from Spain, an airport security man pulled me aside and told me that a whole host of photographers were assembled outside in the arrivals lounge. I was a little nervous, but neither I nor Maria had anything to hide. We boldly stepped out of the customs area awaiting the flashing cameras and prying questions. There wasn't even a flicker from a cigarette lighter and the only question I was asked was by a photographer who enquired as to how I was feeling after being in a clinic. Not one happy snapper took advantage of this golden photo opportunity to sell a cock and bull story to a national about me having an affair. Maria and I just sailed through, I even said hello to a couple I recognised from many a photo call on my garden lawn. One of them asked if I was feeling better after being in the clinic and wished me luck.

The holiday was a well-deserved break for me. I couldn't afford it, but for the next few weeks it helped restore some order into my life and allowed me to get the bulk of my music work finished, thus pleasing a considerable number of waiting clients.

I don't know what made me do it, but one morning I headed off to the off licence to buy a bottle. Nothing could stop me if I wanted a drink. I told myself that I'd been a good boy and I was going to blow it if I bought a drink, but I was just like an arrogant two-year-old determined to get my own way regardless of the consequences.

When I got home, I held the full bottle of whisky up to my mouth and, without stopping, gulped down over half its contents. My whole body tried to throw it back up, but it was too late, the damage had been done and I was back on yet another bender.

Things never, ever got better when I was drinking. I'd wake up in the middle of the night soaking wet, having pissed myself once again. Now, though, I'd got to the stage of not even worrying about that. I'd lay in my wet bed for hours and only move to grasp hold of the bottle sitting on the bedside table. After downing some more booze, I'd fall asleep and wake up with only enough time to get to the local shops to replenish my depleted supplies.

Long gone were the days when I'd travel to three or four shops to buy a bottle at each. I didn't care any more and I would buy two if not three from the same shop.

Everything was done with a drink in my hand. I'd wash and shave with a whisky. I'd even take one into the shower with me and if I had a coffee I'd add some whisky to brighten it up. I'd lie to people on the phone, telling them I'd not touched a drop for some considerable time. But as I spoke with the phone in one hand, there would be a bottle in the other. I didn't go anywhere without a drink. It was my security blanket and I didn't feel safe without it. I'd conceal it in my briefcase and took to wearing suits, as an inside jacket pocket would hold half a bottle with ease, and no one need ever know.

When I tried to ease up or even thought about stopping, the cold turkey effects set in quickly. The only way to ease my suffering was to drink. It stopped me hallucinating and vomiting and it dulled the intolerable pain of my whole body needing to be fed its regular dose of medication.

I felt there was no way out of this mess and I knew deep down that I was on my way out. I just couldn't stop myself. I looked the pits. I'd stopped washing and shaving and I split my limited time awake between the lavatory and the bedroom.

Week after week passed. The next thing I knew was someone asking me for directions as I lay in the back of a car being driven somewhere in London.

I was with Maria and Maria's mother looking for some clinic. In sheer desperation I had asked them to get me into another clinic. My dad had done some homework and found me one as he knew I didn't want to go back to Chesterton Grange.

After a long tour of the city lights, we eventually found the place and I, being slightly over the yardarm, laughed as I was checked in. The procedure was the same as at Chesterton Grange, a Common Entrance exam for all clinics around the world: my bags were checked for illicit substances, a doctor was called and I was requested to stay in my room for fear of mixing with the other patients, as I smelt of drink.

I was given some green and white oblong pills to take, which made me feel drowsy. They were to help restrain the withdrawal symptoms which would soon be affecting my whole body. I was put in an observation room which felt like a fish tank: there was a huge window on one side of the room and every so often someone's eye would appear amongst the slats of the venetian blinds on the other side. I'd peer back, pulling a funny face, and they'd disappear. A consultant came to see me and we chatted for about fifteen minutes about my drinking history. He didn't seem to take much notice but came out with the usual cracking one liner, 'I'll come and see you Monday when I'm sure you'll feel more like talking.' Sod off, I thought. You couldn't have picked a better day to come to a new clinic, Keith! Here we go again. The weekend is to digest and reflect on the past week's activities!

I couldn't remember much about the past week, but I had a memorable weekend. I experienced a new way of administering my much-needed medication. It was with a huge needle stuck into one of the cheeks of my bottom. The miracle wonder drug was aptly named vitamin B. Twice a day this routine was performed and I had to cope with all types of so-called needle experts. One morning there'd be a Tessa Sanderson, a nurse who appeared to shuffle up from a few feet away and thrust the javelin into my buttock, the next it was Eric Bristow the darts champion stepping up to the oche and having to make do with a score of treble one. I felt like a pin cushion.

The clinic's ambience resembled a Holiday Inn hotel. There was very little difference between either of the clinics I'd been in. I attended the same form of group therapy, I was given the same sort of medication and at both places I spent more time in the smoking room than anywhere else. The staff were very pleasant, but no more experienced than others I'd come across. At the time, I felt safer in some form of institution; I was far more secure in a clinic than at home. God only knows what sort of state I'd be in if I was allowed to indulge in my own company.

I made phone calls to my parents and to my sister Janice. Once again, they were with me all the way. They were prepared to spend time chatting and help me in any way they could. I only needed to ask. I also phoned Maggie, who told me she was going to be in London over the weekend and she'd pop in to see me and bring me some clothes.

Apart from Maggie's visit, I spent most of the weekend virtually left to my own devices. I was asked to join in the odd group therapy session and an evening meeting before traipsing off to bed. I was bored. I felt than if I was going to get better I required a little more attention that I was receiving at this new clinic.

Eventually, after I told Maggie how I felt I was being treated, adding a few extra lies about the place, as I usually did, she suggested I go back to Chesterton Grange. I told Maria as well but she, like the rest of the staff at the new clinic, thought I hadn't really given the place a chance. They were right, I hadn't, but I was sick and I made the decision, rightly or wrongly to move.

Maria drove me home to Lime Tree Cottage and the following day Maggie took me back to Chesterton Grange. This time they had found me a bedroom right next to the front door, well away from the other patients. It was a lot quieter than before, but, to be honest, I missed the sounds of the odd patient throwing a wobbly or being given ECT. The occasional yell spiced up the joint and made the new patients wonder whether it would be them who'd next be plugged in to the clinic's mains.

Now I had to go through the laborious process of explaining to every cook, cleaner and counsellor why I was back. I had no excuses left this time, but I was determined to give it my best shot. I knew that it was me who wasn't giving the clinic a chance to help me understand or even cope with my addiction. I'd totally abused the place. During counselling sessions, I'd played games and told them what I wanted them to hear while keeping the real truths to myself. Even when I was asked to tell the group my life story, I gave them the *This is Your Life* Cheggers version, full of anecdotes and a chuckle every so often about the people I'd worked with. This time I contemplated opening up a bit and letting them in to my real world.

On this third visit, there was very little need for me to go back on to a course of drugs. When I told them what I'd already been given, at the other clinic, they were quite content to reduce my medication and maybe top it up with the odd sleeping pill in the evening.

This time round I was even more concerned about the type of people I was boarding with. There was one lady who walked round the corridors with one of those Kiddicraft cassette machines. She'd press the giant play button and out from its crackly speaker would come a selection of church music. Occasionally, you could recognise the odd classic, but most of it was totally inaudible. It was all right having the odd burst at three o'clock in the afternoon, but sometimes she'd give us a rendition at three in the morning. Someone must have either taken her batteries away or given her one or two more sleeping pills, as it stopped after a while. As you might have guessed, she was one of the psychiatric brigade.

On the alkie side of things, I heard that one guy still smelt of booze and appeared to be pissed three days after being admitted into treatment. A huge search went underway to find his secret supply, but, alas, none was found. The only time this chap ever moved out of the clinic was to fetch some cigarettes out of his car which had been left in the car park. I believe one of the nurses caught him not only having a fag by the side of his vehicle but a drink, too. He'd been much more imaginative than all of the rest of us put together. He didn't bother swigging from a bottle, instead he'd hidden his favourite drink in the windscreen wash bottle and was administering his tipple by holding his finger on the applicator inside and guzzling it from the nozzle by the wipers.

I attended group lectures and lessons without fail and found that some counsellors used me like an experimental rat to explain to new patients the importance of staying away from that first drink. I'd argue with the odd newcomer, accusing them of using my old tricks and being in constant denial about their drinking. It wasn't easy to con me any more, I knew the tricks of the trade. I picked holes in my fellow alcoholics' deceptive ways. I felt that by helping them I was also helping myself.

I listened intently to every lecture and made notes on stabilisation and recovery, acute and post withdrawal symptoms. I went to lectures on stress management, rather than trips to the leisure centre and talked openly to the other patients about my recovery plan. Sometimes I was disappointed when lectures were cancelled and we were offered a video to watch. Some patients breathed a sigh of relief at not having to attend another group meeting. Not me. I wanted to learn more.

I was still having a weekly session with Professor Alpen, the German/Austrian hot shot. He told me that he'd made himself a drug addict and an alcoholic. He wanted to endure and experience the sufferings of an addict and by doing so help them to give up. Somehow, he left me unpersuaded.

Most of the other people he'd counselled told me that within only a few sessions they'd given him a full account of their lives. I'd had a number of long sessions with Professor Alpen and, by this stage, I don't think I'd made it past puberty. He always seemed to prefer talking about showbiz.

It was a time for honesty and I took the gamble of telling one of the other counsellors, Val, that I was unhappy with my sessions with Roger Brown. I said that he made me feel uncomfortable and that I wasn't prepared to open up in front of him. It felt like telling tales out of school but fortunately there was no reprimand. She said that she would speak to Roger and for the time being she would take it upon herself to counsel me herself. This made me feel

a lot happier, although things didn't change. I eventually ended up
having sessions with two counsellors.

One lunchtime, Roger came to my room and asked me a lot of
questions about how I was going to cope when I'd left the clinic.
I told him that it was too early to think about any kind of future
and that my immediate concern was coping with controlling my
addiction. He went on about getting someone to move in with me,
maybe an au pair, friend or housekeeper. Eventually, I had to tell
him that I was going to live on my own come rain, hail or shine.

The same evening Maggie came to the clinic as every week
the next of kin were invited to a freebie lecture. It was given
to help the co-dependants understand more about the problems
of alcoholism. How to cope with an alcoholic in the family, an
insight into what they're going through, how the clinic is helping
the alcoholic to deal with their addiction and also how they
might be able to help themselves. If you've had to live with
a drunk for so long, it's bound to affect you in some way or
other.

It was a course of very good informative lectures, which should
really be started from the beginning. Sometimes, however, depending on when the patient was admitted to the clinic, some partners
couldn't wait to attend and would leap head first and join the
course halfway through. Bad move.

If you joined halfway, heaven knows what you might hear. It was
sometimes a bit too much for immediate relatives to be told that
because there was an alcoholic in the family they too had suffered
and they were also ill. The alcoholic had affected them and thus,
had manipulated their general behaviour. They too needed help
and it was all because of the pisshead downstairs.

Naturally, some people would misinterpret what they'd been
told. Even with the utmost care from the lecturer there were
those who just weren't listening.

Like playing a game of charades, when given a film, TV programme or book to describe we all interpret it in our own individual
way and sometimes even forget what charade we were given to
do.

I was lucky that Maggie didn't mix up facts and that she joined
the course at the very beginning. When some spouses heard that
they were ill because of the alcoholic downstairs all sorts of fracas
would take place.

I made a point of being in the smoking room with a newcomer to watch them cope with the couple of hours of waiting for their loved ones to appear after their first ever session.

While the lecture went on upstairs, it was hell for the paranoid alcoholic downstairs, who felt that they were the only subject of debate. I'd watch them light endless cigarettes and sit through a few hours of persecution.

Once the meeting was over, some family and friends would leave without saying goodbye (they hadn't listened) while others who stayed behind only did so for an argument.

This time, while the evening lecture was in full swing I went to my room and contemplated my life in treatment over the next few weeks. What the hell was I doing? I was like a kid back at school. I was a good boy who was looking for a smile from the teacher. I was making all the right moves and I was never late with my homework. I made meticulous notes and filled in recovery plans to read and to please my peers.

Like a child, though, I was getting bored. Once again, I didn't blame myself for my predicament, I instantly condemned the clinic. I was only filling in time, I was getting nowhere, and it was their fault.

I couldn't take it any more. I'd had enough of flitting from one treatment centre to the next and if I had to sit through one more counselling session or another newcomer prattling on about hiding his drink, I'd probably have to ask for a transfer to the psychiatric unit. I tore up all my notes on alcoholism and chucked them in the bin. Once again, I decided to go solo, give up on my own. I never even thought about sleeping on it. I'd made the decision to leave and even before the session upstairs was over I'd already secretly packed my bags and contemplated my departure later the same evening.

I waited until Maggie had gone, then I said my own goodbyes to Chesterton Grange. I told some of my closer friends at the clinic (i.e. nearly all the patients) that I was leaving, but asked them to keep quiet until later on in the evening. I didn't want the staff to get wind of my plan until I was ready. I thought it best to say my fond farewells, after ten o'clock. By that time, most of the clinic's personnel would have gone home and I hoped that no counsellor was going to come back at such a late hour to convince me to stay. Unbeknown to anyone, I'd already booked a cab to drive me home. I told the driver to be waiting outside for me from ten o'clock onwards.

Just before then, having packed my bags, I walked into the nursing station and requested a release form. Each time a patient leaves, some documentation has to be filled in basically saying that the patient is leaving of their own volition.

The duty night nurse thought I was joking, but for once I'd lost that Cheggers smile and very quickly he took on board that I was bloody serious.

One of the nurses called Roger and I was offered the phone to speak to him. I declined the invitation and insisted once more that they produce a release form for me to sign or I would just walk out. Eventually one was found, I signed it and I went to my room to pick up my bags. I was shaking slightly at the time. It was probably the bravest thing I'd done in years but I felt it was right.

To be honest, here I was once again, abusing the clinic and its treatment. Once again I was unprepared to give them a chance of trying to help me. But Clever Dick thought otherwise.

Before leaving, I made a quick call to my mum and dad, brother and sister and told them what I was doing. They didn't try to make me stay in treatment and I asked them to leave me alone for a while. I told them not to call or visit me, just wait for me to get in touch with them. I knew it was difficult for them to understand, but I pleaded for them to steer clear of me for a few months. I promised, like never before, that if they were to wait, they would see a new me on the other side. My mum cried on the phone; I think she knew that this time I wouldn't let her down.

On Wednesday 21 October 1992 I got in my cab and left Chesterton Grange for the last time.

Chapter Nine

When the cab that brought me home from the clinic disappeared down the drive of Lime Tree Cottage I felt elated to be away from all the pressures that had hung over me in treatment. For the first time since I'd decided to do something about my alcoholism, I felt some optimism about my future. It had taken me a long time to realise that the only way I was going to overcome my addiction was to do it myself. I had tried many times before, and failed. Doctors, psychiatrists, counsellors and clinics could only enlighten me as to the problems caused by drinking. They provided me with helpful hints on how to steer clear of that first drink and how to make it through a day. But even on that first night home I contemplated having a drink. Then I remembered the saying, 'If you don't have a drink you can't get drunk'. There was no booze in the house, so I forced myself to go to bed, to stop my brain ticking ten to the dozen. I tossed and turned all night and only managed a few hours' sleep.

I spent the next morning in my recording studio trying to patch up some unfinished music tracks that I'd promised a client for some time. I hadn't had the nerve to speak to him before going away to the funny farm and thought that by producing the tapes, albeit rather long after the deadline, I could still hope to receive some payment.

Shortly after eleven, the phone rang. I knew it wasn't going to be from one of my family, but it was the call I'd been expecting. It was Roger from the clinic. Each sentence seemed to take an age to complete as he droned on about how he thought I hadn't given the clinic a chance and how I should have stayed a while longer. Eventually, I agreed to go back for the odd aftercare session. It was one way of getting him off the phone and letting me get on with my own way of becoming sober. I didn't want to upset him too much as I thought it may be useful to keep a foot in the clinic's door in case of any major relapse.

Two days out of the clinic and I hadn't touched a drink. I'd filled up the fridge with bottles of mineral water, tubs of cottage cheese and chicken pieces. I lived on chocolate, tins of fruit and rice pudding. They were the only foods I could eat at the time, as anything else seemed to play havoc with my stomach, and over a short period I managed to lose some of the weight I'd put on through drink.

Time, they say, is the greatest healer, but what they don't tell you is that you've also got to fill it. Days seemed to drag by. At the clinic they suggest filling in some of the hours with a bit of light exercise, some reading and plenty of sleep. In reality, what I found most useful was loads of telly watching and eating tons of chocolate. The only exercise I did was to lift a glass of mineral water to my lips.

I'd sweat and panic as I watched the twenty-four hour clock on the video machine tick past closing time at the off licence. Once the witching hour had gone, I knew it would be at least eight hours before any shop locally would be open where I could buy a bottle. Those eight hours seemed like an endurance test. I'd go to bed late and try to sleep. I'd doze off for an hour, wake up in a cold sweat and look at my watch to see how long it was before I could breathe again. For some unknown reason, I felt more at ease during the day with the knowledge that there was someone somewhere who would sell me a drink if I really needed one. I began to live in fear of the long nights when all was closed.

I felt that I needed some extra help. It was pointless asking a mate to come over, so I made my own decision to go to an AA meeting and for the first time it was with no real encouragement from anyone else. The meeting helped me fill in a few hours of that day, but after two hours of hearing about everyone else's problems, I still wasn't convinced that a room full of drunks was going to stop me.

I'd made friends with a number of them and I even found myself giving the select few my home number after the meeting. In return, they gave me theirs and suggested that if I needed someone to speak to, at any time of the day, I should just pick up the phone and call. When I got home those numbers went straight into the bin. I was taken up with the obsession that, if I was going to stop, it was going to be me alone that would do it. I didn't want to air my laundry with a stranger. No one could help me with my plight.

I have to admit I was really struggling. I so desperately wanted to drink again, yet at the same time I wanted to make people aware of how well I was doing. I wanted recognition, a pat on the back and praise for being such a good boy. I decided to go to one of the after care meetings at Chesterton Grange.

One Saturday morning I set off in my car. Roger wasn't normally there at the weekends, but I knew that if I went to the clinic word would get back to him of my well-being. Even if no one during my visit said Well done, the thought of him knowing I was going straight was enough to satisfy my own ego.

It was one of those weekend hold-hands-and-wake-up-the-dead kind of group therapy meetings. My turn came to tell the group how I was feeling and, by God, did I let them have it. I must have prattled on for a good ten minutes about how wonderful life was just one leap over the hedge and outside the walls of the clinic. I told the group, newcomers and all, that I'd never felt better. By the end of my deliberation I could have filled the whole of my car including the boot with patients willing to come and live a life like mine.

As a matter of fact, it did cross my mind at one stage to open up my home as a treatment centre. What alcoholics needed, I thought, was a bit of tender loving care, the odd lecture (which could be read from a text book) and one of those large easels with a set of big pens. Counselling would be a doddle. At each session, when chatting to a patient, I would emulate my peers. I would wear a suit, scratch the back of my neck and cross my legs occasionally. To act with some authority and relay to the patient I was in touch with their feelings, I would formulate my next question by using the last few words of their own sentence and throwing it back at them. For example: Patient: 'I had a terrible night'. Counsellor: 'A terrible night?' Patient: 'Yes, I dreamt I was drinking again'. Counsellor [has to add a few words]: 'Oh dear! Drinking again'. And so on. Fill in forty minutes with waffle, guarantee another chat in seven days and Weyhey! I was sure I could make a small fortune.

My session was over. On the way home from the clinic I contemplated stopping to buy a drink, but I fought with myself and tried to make it through yet another day. It was such hard work, especially when I got home and had bugger all to do, no one to talk to, and no incentive to do anything.

I spent the rest of the weekend gasping for a drink. My saving grace was that Maggie had invited me to go bowling with herself and Rose. The thought of seeing them again arrested my need to buy a bottle. I enjoyed my time with them. I laughed a lot, especially at Rose who was trying to wreck the bowling lane by throwing the bowl like a shotputter.

The following day, I was invited to take Rose and her friends to the cinema. This glimmer of light in what was now a heavy period of my life was keeping me away from that first drink. We went to see Walt Disney's *Beauty and the Beast* with four hundred other kids about the same age as Rose. The cinema was jam packed with mums and dads playing Find the four-year-old, with the house lights down and the film rolling on regardless.

Rose asked to go to the loo during all the important plot-setting scenes and the arguments with the other kids in our party over whose popcorn was whose were unbearable. Most kids when watching Disney films try to copy the characters on screen. With so much hassle and so many toddlers running riot, it was obvious that very few kids had seen Beauty as most of them were emulating the Beast.

I made it past the weekend, but sadly no further. I'd convinced myself I'd done enough and I bought a bottle. Once again, I'd made a promise to myself to take control over my drinking and for the next three days I'd managed to stay on an even keel. But once again I'd succumbed.

My agent phoned with some work. He offered me the opportunity to go on the television programme *This Morning* and talk about the pressures of a life in show business. I didn't particularly want to travel all the way up to Liverpool and talk about something which I knew was a lie. I told him I'd think about it, which normally meant, I don't want to do it but I haven't thought of an excuse yet.

He also told me about an enquiry for a new television series on the ITV network. They wouldn't tell me anything about the programme, except that it was a game show, I was on the shortlist and they'd like to see me in a week's time. I was so excited and I knew I had at least seven days to get my act together. I'd use the same system as of old and drink only Night Nurse for a few days before the audition. I was convinced that I was the right man for the job. Everything was coming right for me again. I was at home, I was seeing Rose and Maggie and now here I was with a series in the offing that I was bound to get.

I drank like never before. As was always my way when I had something promising to look forward to, I thought I could stop a few days before, sober up and give the job my best shot. It never, *ever* worked. I was heading for a repeat performance of what had happened before.

I was once asked to audition for the stage show *Me and My Girl* in the West End. Days before, I eased up and drank my Night Nurse so I would be on top form for the audition. For hours I practised the song 'Leaning on a Lamp Post' in front of the mirror and even got out my tap shoes to brush up on my dancing.

I was all set for the big day and had organised a car to drive me to and from London. With only a few hours to go before my departure, I decided to give myself a confidence booster. I took more than a sip from my bottle of whisky, drinking well over half its contents. Whilst all dressed up and waiting to leave, I practised my song and rehearsed my tap routine on the stone floors of the house. As I tapped I had a glass of whisky in my hand. After every rigorous run-through I awarded myself another drink.

I can hardly remember the knock on the door from my cab driver. I believe I slept all the way into Town. He tried to wake me en route, but I was well and truly out of it. Once he got to Heathrow Airport he did a U-turn and drove me, tap shoes and all, back home. I can only thank him for not letting me go to the audition in that state.

What a surprise that I never made it to the audition for the new television series as I'd spent the previous week celebrating my return to showbusiness. I went out and bought enough booze for a party. I drank all day and all night. I don't know which days came and went, who phoned or knocked at my front door and I didn't care. I spent all of my time in bed, waking only to guzzle from my bottle.

The next thing I remember was struggling in some posh hotel trying to get washed and dressed and look a little more presentable for my debut on Britain's most popular morning programme . . .

CHAPTER TEN

It was now ten o'clock on 5 November 1992. I stared at the television in the hospitality room at Albert Dock studios in Liverpool. I thought about what questions Richard and Judy might ask me. I smiled inside and wondered, if I had been asked to do a similar interview on Radio One, whether a researcher for the show would ask me to think of a few amusing anecdotes to capture the listener's attention.

I was taken down to the studio for the start of the programme. On the way, I talked to a studio floor assistant; I'd decided that it was the right thing to get it all over with. I couldn't hide my problem any more and it was too late to just walk away from the programme.

I was worried about what people would think of me. I'd read those stories in the papers before: 'Magistrate Seen with Hooker', 'Street Star Accused of Taking Drugs'. I wondered whether people's perceptions of me would change, that some folk would ridicule me, take the piss.

I thought it best to be totally up front, tell the truth. I wanted no more skeletons in my cupboard and I didn't want it all to drag on for years and years. I don't think I really embarrassed anyone by my behaviour. I didn't encourage others to participate in my antics. I hadn't mugged an old lady. I hadn't run anyone over or robbed a bank. I just drank, although admittedly I drank a lot.

I had been told at my meetings to take things 'one day at a time'. I now felt that I knew what that expression really meant and it was time to use it. Get today over and done with and worry about the rest later. Now I had a golden opportunity to get the story straight, tell it how it was and let people in general make up their own minds.

I was sitting in a chair ready for the interview. A sound engineer fiddled with my microphone. Lots of things I'd been told began to make sense. Like a huge jigsaw puzzle, I was piecing it all together only moments before the show.

Part of getting sober·is being honest. When you admit to yourself and others that you have a problem then you're on your way to getting some control back into your life. I was just about to take a massive first step on my road to sobriety.

For the first time ever on live TV I talked honestly and openly about myself. For years during any newspaper, radio or television interview, I had told people what I thought they wanted to hear, the odd gag, amusing story and chat about how wonderful life was and what future projects I had coming up. This time I had nothing to brag about, but I felt I was doing something much more constructive than being the usual Keith Chegwin.

Richard and Judy were marvellous. Before the show started they put me at my ease. I felt I was in the hands of two of the most caring, professional and genuine presenters in the country.

My heart pounded as the titles of the show ran. I looked at my hands and they were shaking. I had a touch of adrenalin, nerves, sweating and withdrawal symptoms all at once. What a combination. I hadn't even had the chance to tell my mum and dad I would be on, nor had I set the video to watch it later.

Richard and Judy welcomed the viewers to the programme and trailed the fact that I would be on the show to talk about my battle with drink. As they spoke I was grateful for a large fan that blew cool air in my direction. I'd often wondered why Judy's hair blew in the wind; I thought a studio door must have been left open during hot days. Now I knew and that fan was my saving grace. It helped me to stop sweating and gave the impression to the viewer I was at least sober.

After the trails for the morning, Richard and Judy's attention turned to me. My speech was somewhat staggered, I repeated myself and I coughed a lot. For those that knew me, the odd cough, I believe, was an instant give away that I'd been drinking.

Mercifully, there were no hard hitting questions. Richard and Judy conducted a careful and well constructed interview and, thanks to their genuine interest in my problem, I was able to be frank and open about my addiction to drink.

The phone lines at Granada Television, I was told, were jammed with well wishers. One person phoned in to say 'I couldn't stand you on TV until now.' I told the nation I was an alcoholic and I left them to make up their own minds about me as I answered each question as honestly as I could. Reference was made to the fact that I'd only been sober for a few months and I let it go. I found the interview rather taxing as I was still feeling a little worse for wear. As I spoke, I regretted getting rat arsed the night before such an important television interview.

After my appearance on the programme, the phone at home never stopped. Maggie even phoned to congratulate me and, although I think she knew I'd been drinking, she never let on. The national papers were never off the phone or away from the house. They pried into my past life within hours of my being on the programme, but to no avail.

The *People* even tried to drum up some extra material about me going out with a woman who worked for a local newspaper. She'd interviewed me some some months back about a local charity fête I'd opened. Since then, I was supposed to have taken her out for dinner and she had also been my guest at a charity ball. The lady in question phoned me at home, as she too was being hounded by reporters. I advised her to tell the truth. Nothing ever came of it as the story was total fabrication and they went away.

To be honest, there wasn't anything else. Some journalists did a pub crawl of my locals without success. Between them they probably consumed more than I ever did at any local hostelry. I was a secret drinker, not one to be found propping up the bar, the butt of everyone's jokes who needed a lift home at the end of the evening.

I felt a bit of a fraud, what with all this reverence going on about how well I'd done to stop. Little were people aware of my binge just hours before my appearance. Nor were they aware that during the interview I was still suffering its effects. I personally still had a long way to go. I hadn't overcome the biggest hurdle of all. Which was to genuinely stop drinking.

This time, I'd created the situation myself and there was no way out. If one newspaper man had crossed the threshold of my house that day, it would have been obvious to him that there was something not quite right with my cover story.

In the breakfast room stood two half-finished bottles of whisky for all to see. The kitchen was awash with glasses and bottles, as though there had been a student's party the night before. The bedroom was even worse. It reeked of stale piss and there were bottles lying on the floor next to the bed. Here was I acting like an angel when behind closed doors there were still enough bottles of booze to invite the entire cast of *Eastenders* round for a party.

I placed my dog Hollie in the driveway outside and, like the good friend she was, she barked if anyone came near the property.

During her quiet moments, I beavered away inside and outside of the farmhouse, clearing away all the incriminating evidence. I searched jacket pockets, cupboards, wardrobes, behind curtains, under beds, carpets and behind toilet cisterns, clearing away the empty and sometimes full or half-consumed bottles of whisky. I took my studio apart and managed to fill box after box with empties, hiding them under old horse blankets in the barn. I checked all the guttering and cleared a few bottles from the garden. Once my work was complete, I was able to relax and consider what my next move should be.

It was now an impossibility for me to go out and buy anything alcoholic to drink. So I had to make do with the circumstances as they stood. I'd had my last drink. I became worried and nervous about the next few days and had this compelling urge to get out of the house. It was getting late and I hadn't prepared anything for the evening, I had to go shopping. Everything had to be perfect. I was like a soldier about to do battle; I was preparing myself for the fight of my life.

I went to the local Tesco and stocked my trolley with loads of bottled water, chocolate and things that were easy for me to eat. Whilst I was there, I became aware that some people in the supermarket were watching my every move. One lady followed me round and at one point I thought she might have been a store detective. After going down the tinned fruit section of the store, I made a quick dash right and sharp right again to see if she would continue her pursuit. She did. I surprised even myself when I ended up in the wine and lager section. I moved my trolley out of that shopping aisle like Nigel Mansell, just in case she was a journalist.

I was stopped by a young couple who'd seen me on television that morning. I awaited their disapproving reaction to the whole episode. Instead, I was treated to a pat on the back and their best wishes. I nearly cried as I finished off my shopping. They'd said, 'Well done, Cheggers,' but I felt as if I'd already let them down.

On the way home I went to the video shop and hired three films. I was scared. I even wondered what would happen if the television failed me that night. I unpacked my shopping, fed Hollie and lay down to sleep on the sofa. I was exhausted.

After less than an hour I woke up. Sheer panic had well and truly set in. It felt like someone had put a plastic bag over my head, I couldn't breathe and the whole of the inside of my body wanted to get out. I raced to the back door so as to get some fresh air and breathe properly again. At the same time, I was shaking, sweating, and vomiting. I was in such a state.

Hollie had stayed with me and as usual she'd found a stone which she wanted me to throw. Bloody dog. Looking back, I thank Hollie for all those times she helped me to take my mind off things. Giving up drink was so difficult for me to do, yet throwing a stone was so simple and it helped ease all my pending stress and anxieties.

Gradually I came round but now I feared having to go back into the house and trying to sleep. I stared into the blackness of the night sky and wondered when all this would be over. When would I feel better? How long would it be before I could have just one good night's sleep? When would the tremendous urge for a drink disappear? I knew that I still had a very long way to go.

I stayed up most of the night thinking about the future. I felt that for the present it was important to organise one personal interview with one of the Sunday papers. I had no preference as to which paper had such an 'exclusive', but I felt it was best to give the story to one, so as not to be pestered by all the others.

I decided to go with the *Sunday Mirror*. The journalist whom my agent had spoken to seemed to take an interest in the problem and was keen to listen to my story rather than come along with a typed questionnaire to be filled in by me. My gut reaction and intuition served me well. The interview appeared that Sunday word for word. It was probably the first interview I'd done in years where the reporter hadn't turned up with a tape machine. He was from the old school of hacks and his experience was certainly made clear to me when I read the article in the paper. Unlike my interview and pictures for *Hello* magazine, the *Sunday Mirror* paid me some much needed money for the story, which kept me going for a while.

The mail poured in with letters of encouragement from all over the country and I can't thank people enough for all their kind sentiments. Replying to all the mail took up a considerable amount of my time, but I was so grateful to people for writing I replied to each and every one of them individually. I even phoned some of the people personally to thank them for the advice and tips they'd given to help me through such a difficult time.

I'd started to use the phone again now but found that I was sadly losing some very close friends ever so quickly. Some would pretend to be out or not return my calls or make see-through excuses for not meeting me. Some of the more renowned stars, understandably, steered clear for fear of the adverse publicity and some who weren't in the limelight I can only assume didn't think it wise to mix with a known drunk.

These supposed friends have recently tried to re-establish contact. But, to be honest, I feel I've come a long way in my search for a better life and lifestyle and during that arduous journey I've made some genuine friends whom I truly appreciate. Not for what they are but for who they are.

Days after appearing on *This Morning* I was still fighting off drink. On more than one occasion I contemplated popping down to the off licence and grabbing a bottle to ease the relentless pain which appeared to have taken over all parts of my body. I was invited to lunch on the Sunday with some of the people that I'd met during my local AA meetings and someone who had also tried to help me on many occasions in the early days when I thought I wanted to stop drinking. She was married, so her husband was used to the odd person in recovery coming round for a chat. I've never met such a lovely couple and they have now become very close friends. I brought them up to date on the situation as it stood. They'd seen my appearance on TV and had guessed that I was still drinking as they'd heard me stumble over my words and give the odd tell-tale cough. They were great company and didn't mind that I couldn't face eating or that I spent a considerable amount of time heaving in their loo in between bouts of diarrhoea.

I didn't fully understand why, and I still don't, but things were at last starting to come together. I knew that if I could cope with the next few weeks and get through the physical trauma of not drinking, I had a chance of making it. It appeared there were lots of people on my side.

Every night I went to meetings with fellow alcoholics. I was taken to some in London, Oxford and the surrounding area. I heard stories from young and old and realised that if I wanted to get better I had to work at it. There was no point in being a martyr, I had no banner to carry. It was honesty that was going to make me well.

I started to tell people who were close to me at the time how I was really feeling. If I was troubled, I'd pick up the phone and speak to someone at three, sometimes four in the morning. Every time I reached out there was always someone there to grab my hand and pull me back out from the mess or sticky situation I'd got myself into. It especially helped me when panic had set in and there seemed only one way out, which was to have a drink. In those harassing circumstances I'd call for help and it was never refused.

I was finding it easier to speak now to those who'd been through similar circumstances to me. In other words, speak to a mechanic about fixing your car, not a hairdresser. One of the blokes I met reminded me of the time he'd popped over to my house to help and ended up chasing me round the garden in the middle of the night. How I'd phoned someone else using the name Kevin and how I'd regularly ring him and shout expletives down the phone.

There were a few Bible bashers around and some people who treated the place like a classroom. Some went to great lengths to complete the first part of the course in the hope of picking up a medal, but in the main, they were just normal folk who, like me, were trying to stay sober. It amazed me how no one was ever turned away. Lots of people came in to those rooms smelling of drink but they were never shown the door. Some told horrendous stories about the things they'd done, but no one was ever ridiculed or condemned for their activities. Everyone mucked in to help one another and some were very willing to go a long way to help a fellow alcoholic stay sober.

It's one thing getting well in a treatment centre for six weeks. But I felt that, to survive, I needed that bit of extra help and I found it at those meetings. It appeared that there was always someone there, if necessary, twenty-four hours a day. If I was going to get myself straight, that's exactly what I needed.

Alcoholics Anonymous doesn't prescribe drugs or attempt clever counselling. A meeting is just a bunch of drunks getting together to sort out their common problem. They gave me a helping hand and it was surprisingly easy to use the information I was given.

With some careful guidance I was just about coping. I thought a lot about drink, but whenever I felt myself being drawn towards the local shop, I would call a mate who would talk me out of it. Within a few weeks, I was actually feeling physically better. I didn't always wake in the middle of the night in a state of panic.

My body was still aching and I was still in danger of throwing up without notice, but slowly and surely the physical effects of wanting a drink were beginning to wane.

My agent called to inform me that a few of my personal appearances had been cancelled. One promoter phoned up to cancel his carol concert. I was more than happy not to turn up to his singalong, so long as he fulfilled his part of the contract and paid me some money for not being there. He changed his mind then but I did notice on my arrival at the venue that there was a complimentary tray of tea and coffee in my dressing room.

My Christmas panto in Aldershot was also in jeopardy. I would have been willing to step down if necessary, but the panto people decided to give me the benefit of the doubt. I guess they hoped that my name, as Buttons in *Cinderella*, would still put bums on seats.

Surprisingly, it did. The theatre was packed. During rehearsals a few opening numbers had to be changed. 'Roll Out the Barrel' probably wasn't the best opening number and 'Tea for Two' only focused the audience's attention on my drink problem. I'm sure a lot of people turned up in the hope that I'd appear on stage pissed, but I never let the producers down. Five weeks after I made my decision, I was still sober and as each day went by I grew stronger.

Mind you, parts of my body were disappearing. I got dreadful toothache and one day as I tucked into some soup and a bread roll one of my bottom teeth just fell out. For the first time in eight years, I called my dentist. He, like the rest of the world, knew about my addiction to alcohol. As he looked into my mouth, I knew that drinking had taken its toll; before I left the chair he managed to remove a few more teeth and replace some others with caps.

Through drink, it felt as though my whole body had fallen apart and it was only time that would put me back together again. I knew that my liver could repair itself, but what about the rest of me? I thought about having a medical, but to this day I haven't bothered, just in case I'm in for some bad news.

By this time I had come to terms with the fact that Maggie and I had no future together. Before now I still thought that there might be a chance. For more time than was just, I clutched at straws; it was difficult for me to let go of old ideals and ideas. However, finally, a mate asked me if I was likely to get the relationship back one hundred per cent. After a lot of careful thought, it became clear to me that there was no way our relationship could ever be redeemed. Over the years we'd grown apart and Maggie now appeared to be happy. It was only fair to let her go and get on with her new independent future. We'd been through a lot together and I'd now come through it a different person. I'd also become more independent and I wanted to get on with my new life in the sober lane. Now our only common interest was Rose and her future. Between us, we decided that Rose was going to live with Maggie and that I would see Rose as much as I wanted.

It was a tough time for all of us. A divorce was well and truly underway and Maggie and I had decided to sell Lime Tree Cottage and use the money to buy our own smaller properties. We came to an amicable decision about who was to have what pieces of furniture when the house was eventually sold.

The press had been trying to catch us both unawares since we announced our separation way back in September. They were even willing to pay large sums of money for our individual stories. But both of us, for Rose's sake, made the decision there was no way they were going to use us in a game of journalistic ping pong. Enough was enough.

During this time, I started to see more and more of Maria. She'd given up working nine to five for her father in December and was looking for some other type of work which would take her out of an office and also give her some independence. I knew that she had enjoyed working for Maggie and myself for nearly seven years, but in the later days, when my drinking was at its height, she had left because she couldn't take it any more.

Maria at this time knew me better than anyone. I would tell her everything, as I knew I could confide in her and not find it splashed across the national newspaper or hear it in a local shop the following day. I told her some very personal things that I was too embarrassed to tell my family about. My panic attacks and how, when they came, I would rush out of the house or hide under the duvet or in a corner. How I'd spend hours living in fear of the postman coming up the drive and having to speak to him. How, every time the phone rang, I'd sweat and fear who was at the other end. How, when I was driving, I'd have to stop the car and throw up on the side of the road. I told her about the people I feared and those I wanted to steer clear of. She also knew that I was desperate to sell the old house. There were too many drinking memories there and every time I went home, flashbacks of my old lifestyle would flit before me. Each room had a story to tell. I felt uncomfortable in its surroundings. I wanted to move to somewhere I could start again.

It was Maria who spotted a house for sale in the local paper. It needed quite a bit of work doing to it but it was only a few miles away from where Rose and Maggie were living. When I went to view the house, the people who owned it told me more than a few times that it was their weekend retreat. I think they were surprised to hear that something so small was to be my home.

Eventually a buyer for our old house was found and on 2 April 1993 I moved into my new home.

Maria had been around at the weekends for the last three or four months as Maggie and I had agreed that when I had Rose, someone else should be there in my early days of sobriety to put her mind at ease. I was willing, for the short term, to go along with this deal to ease any tension that was looming with the sale of the house and the divorce.

Maria had seen me at my best and my worst and she, like a few other good mates, was there for me, willing to help in any way she could. After the panto had finished, I started to get on really well with her. When I was asked to attend a function or a dinner party with friends, I'd ask Maria to come as my partner. It didn't concern me that other people thought there might be something going on, as it was well over a year since Maggie had made up her mind to seek a divorce. Maria became the stumbling block for any journo that tried to contact me and I even asked her to handle any deals that came through my agent. I think she understood that I had enough problems coping with my sobriety, that the last thing I needed was anything else to upset the applecart.

The need to earn some money was paramount. I'd always said that I would be willing to drive a bus to earn some money and now I found that job search was only one step away. I decided to make contact with a few mates at the BBC. I hadn't been in touch with them for a long time and wondered what was going on in the respected media centre of the world. Not a lot. However, I went to lunch with one of them who was in charge of selling merchandise. He was into selling licensed BBC keyrings and diaries, *East Enders* beermats and mugs and had even procured the rights to sell Mr Blobby T-shirts. He asked me whether I'd be keen to get involved in a few merchandising deals. I was quick to accept and found myself as a sales rep approaching large corporations in the hope of selling them the odd T-shirt. I enjoyed acting the part of the businessman. I'd bought a double sized executive briefcase, I had a portable phone and I always dressed in a suit and tie to look the part.

Once I was having lunch at the BBC when I was approached by one of my old bosses who enquired what TV show I was there to present. When I told him I was there flogging T-shirts he went away with a chuckle and it was obvious that he thought I was joking. After a few months, though, I had to admit defeat as I was working on a commission basis. It appeared that all my hard work wasn't enough to produce the cost of a bacon butty. So I thought it best to give up the job.

As far as the entertainment business was concerned, I found that I was regularly being asked to appear on television shows as the expert on drink. I was asked to appear in drinking videos and to speak on the subject at great length in magazines. All of which I turned down. I didn't want to talk about it any more. I, and I'm sure the general public, were fed up with hearing about my drink problem. I didn't want to become the celebrity drunk who was dragged out each Christmas to talk about drink driving or become the expert on a panel for *The Time . . . The Place*. I wanted my career back. I wanted to get up on stage and do an hour's cabaret, open a shop or even present a programme.

My chance came, though somewhat alarmingly, when I was asked to present an Eighties pop quiz on a programme called *The Word*, a late-night Friday evening show on Channel Four known for its no-holds-barred style of presentation and interviews. I'd seen many a celebrity thrown by their unusual line of questioning. The programme lived off its sensationalism, and here was I being asked to be a guest and also host part of the show.

I called in all the experts. Some of my best friends advised me to steer clear. The programme was bound to take the piss out of chirpy Cheggers and his days on *Swap Shop* and *Cheggers Plays Pop*. I was great material for any alternative presenter.

I phoned my sister Janice, as it was always her opinion I respected most. She put me right and told me that I had nothing to lose. Now that I'd got my act together I could give as good as I got if any confrontational situation arose. However, she did add that I should seriously look at my wardrobe and consider getting something to wear that was a little bit more up-to-date than my drab selection of suits and ties.

All my attention was focused on this one appearance on TV. Maria and I set off for the shops on the King's Road in London. Whilst I browsed through the golfing sweaters in some shops, Maria produced some outrageous outfits from the back of others. We came across a suit which was more than my budget could really accommodate, but we decided it was worth it, to create the desired effect, the new-look Keith Chegwin. It was a simple black, but classy suit which made me look as though I had some street cred.

I wasn't too concerned about my interview on the show as I would have no control over that part of the programme. But I took loads of time and careful thought on how to present the quiz I'd been asked to host. It was a simple question-and-answer format using members of the studio audience and testing their knowledge of the Eighties. I rehearsed every question on the script I'd been sent over and over again so that I wouldn't stumble on the day. Before leaving home, I made sure I'd packed my presenter's earpiece and headed off for rehearsals only hours before the show went out live.

At the runthrough there were many changes to the running order, but I found all the old presenter tricks came back quickly. Camera changes and moves, people talking in my earpiece as I rehearsed the item were not a problem. I even filled in time by ad libbing when I spied that they weren't quite ready for the next item in rehearsals.

Rehearsals had gone well and I was ready for the live programme at eleven in the evening. The studio audience was let on to the studio floor half an hour before the programme started. Half of them had just come out of the pub and there seemed to be no one there who was over the age of twenty-one. I would have felt much happier with an older audience, at least a group of pensioners weren't going to shout out 'tosser' when I walked on the set.

Mark Lamarr was hosting the programme that night and I sat opposite as he introduced me. As he said my name, a roar went up from the studio audience. I presumed they were taking the micky! The embarrassing cheers went on for what seemed an age as Mark tried to get a word in edgeways. As they cheered I wondered whether maybe there were a few people in that studio audience who actually liked me. It made me laugh as it was totally unexpected. It gave me such a boost, I felt elated.

Mark's line of questioning wasn't as tough as I'd expected and even he admitted after the show that his original questions had gone to the wall after such a reaction. Thank you, Mark. I hosted the quiz and enjoyed every minute of being back on television. I was on a high. I liked being with television people and I got a great kick out of doing 'seat of your pants' live TV.

After the programme had finished I was thanked by Paul Ross, producer of the show. Then he and the executive producer, Charlie Parsons, asked if I'd like to present some outside broadcasts for Channel Four's morning programme *The Big Breakfast*. I leapt at the offer, although at that time I hadn't seen the show. On the way home, I wondered whether it was one of those hospitality promises that would be all forgotten in the morning.

The only other television commitment I had coming up was for an ITV children's programme called *Go Getters*. It was a challenge series that I'd been asked to take part in every year since it started. Nine celebrities and their TV crews took to the road for five days and had to complete three tasks per day which could be anything from wing walking to deep sea diving. I really loved the show and I liked the company of the stars that appeared on it. They, like the crew, were willing to give up a whole week to work on it.

I was surprised that no one had phoned to cancel my appearance on the series. Not that the producers of the show wouldn't want to use me, but that the hierarchy for the ITV network may not want to use someone for a kid's show who'd had so much publicity for drinking.

I called the producer at home. He was a friend, so I confided in him saying I would fully understand if they didn't want to use me. I was expecting him to thank me for the call and say he'd been wondering how to approach me and tell me the bad news. Instead, he said that if I wasn't going to be on the show nor was he. I made a promise to him that if he wanted me to appear on *Go Getters* ever again, I would drop everything to make myself available.

A month passed and I was still waiting for the call from *The Big Breakfast* about doing a week on the show. I thought about calling them but, although I was desperate to work, I held back for a few more weeks.

Eventually, the phone call came and I was asked to appear on the show for the week of 12 April 1993. It was one of the most exciting periods of my life and I can't thank the people on the programme enough. I'd spent the last three years fighting drink. My whole life had centred around a bottle of Bells and no one, understandably, had trusted me. No one had given me a chance as I'd always managed to screw things up. Yet here I was, for the first time in a long while, with people who were fully aware of my past being allowed to appear, not for a few minutes, but for a whole week on one of Britain's top television shows.

They must have spent some time in the office contemplating such a difficult decision. Could I be trusted? Would I let them down? Would they have to apologise to the nation if I didn't appear one morning? They were really taking a gamble as they wouldn't know whether they'd find me pissed out of my head lying next to a mini bar in a hotel room until moments before the show.

I packed my street cred gear and prepared for a week on the road. My job on the show was to knock on the public's front door and get them out of their houses to join in some *Big Breakfast* antics, which could be anything from jumping for money on trampolines to competing in an egg-and-spoon race with a neighbour.

The week before, I watched and recorded every programme from start to finish so I could get to grips with my role. The whole programme appeared to be very chaotic and haphazard, changing from one day to the next. It was a brand new era of television which I had yet to experience.

My first outside broadcast was in Knaresborough in Yorkshire. I was asked to go down a street and ask the residents to come out of their houses for a hoe-down with a country and western band at seven in the morning. I presumed that all these doorstep hits were pre-arranged. I thought that houses had probably been leafleted the night before and a researcher had spoken to the residents to find some likely fun members of the public for me to wake. But no. I was about to experience how live TV can really be.

In the old days I'd have been working with a crew of at least twelve to fourteen people, but our crew consisted of a producer, a cameraman and myself. Just before going live a couple of satellite engineers turned up with a huge dish to beam the pictures out to the nation. I asked my producer which house had been selected for me to go to. He said there hadn't and, not only that, where we were standing was streets away from where I was going to be knocking. It was genuinely all a big surprise, not only for me, but for the people whose doors I was to knock on.

I felt like Roger Cook as I ran down the street and woke up the neighbourhood. To my amazement, the general public were more than willing to let me into their homes with a camera. That week they came out for a hoe-down, took part in silly competitions and I was even let on to a houseboat with a group of Sea Scouts to give the vessel a spring clean. It was real ad lib television and such fun. By the end of the week my agent was on the phone to me and I believe a deal had been struck to sign me up for a two-year period.

I couldn't believe it, I was so lucky. There had been a time when I thought I'd never work on television again and here I was, back on mainstream television six months after my appearance on *This Morning*. I was delighted.

CHAPTER ELEVEN

I'd been asked to start full time on *The Big Breakfast* later on in the year and it was all down to Janice and my appearance on *The Word*.

With the knowledge that I had a major contract coming up I was happy to try and struggle through financially until my work started. It was still a rough time for me as not a day went by when I didn't think about drink. My senses seemed to be heightened, like a fox when he runs across unknown terrain. He stops, looks around and takes in his surroundings until he's familiar with them. Like him, I became more and more aware as the days went by that alcohol seemed to be everywhere. It was in shops, supermarkets, houses, work places, on trains, boats and planes and even in hotel bedrooms as a thank you for choosing to stay at that particular Inn. There was no getting away from it.

The first thing people seemed to ask me on my arrival anywhere was, 'What would you like to drink?' At first, I avoided any situation that involved me being confronted with booze. After six months of sobriety, I still didn't feel safe and I didn't trust myself. When drink was around, I could smell it like warm bread in a bakery. Warm and inviting and it was there tempting me all the time.

On those rare and dangerous moments, I would have no hesitation but to get up and leave. Some people objected to my early departure from dinner parties or the invitation to stay up late in a hotel for a chinwag. But I knew that if I stayed, temptation might have got the better of me and I could easily start up my old tricks again.

Many a time I would sit in a hotel bedroom and the mini bar would stare back. I had the key to that house of horrors, the key that would set me off on that endless wheel of ducking, diving, lying, cheating and sheer desperation to get my next cocktail. Some nights I found it so difficult to sleep I'd get up and open the door to the mini bar and stare back at it. It helped me to remember the bad times. Eventually I'd calm down and close the door, just like I had on my drinking.

I still hadn't had a full night's sleep. I'd sometimes shake uncontrollably in bed and have the feeling that I was being crushed in a huge vice. I was still frightened of sleeping as I knew I would lay there for hours tossing and turning, sweating and thinking of past, present and future. I never thought of such things when I had a bottle beside the bed. If I stirred during the night a few long gulps from it assured me of a few hours' extra sleep until it was time to start another day of boozing.

Now I'd nod off and then wake at two or three o'clock in the morning, bright as a button, mind buzzing and body raring to go. I eventually asked a friend for help. I phoned him at two o'clock in the morning to find him still awake. I told him about what I was going through night after night. I also enquired why he was up so late. He told me that after eight years of sobriety not one night had gone by when he didn't wake up or have problems with his sleep. Many's the time he'd been tempted to pour himself a big one and go back to bed.

After our long chat I felt slightly more at ease, lying there in my bed content in the knowledge that I wasn't alone, there must be thousands of poor sods going through the same ordeal. They say that no one ever died through lack of sleep, but after three days of it you sometimes feel like committing suicide. I've stopped drinking coffee, orange juice and eating chocolate in the evenings and, if I do have to get up, I usually find that a piece of toast and a glass of warm milk help me relax enough to go back to bed and catch a couple of hours.

Maria and I were getting on really well now. We'd dine together, go to the cinema together and some nights I'd ask her to stay. I eventually asked her to move in with me and she agreed. She knew how difficult things were at the time and left me to my own devices; she knew that all I wanted was to get better. She never questioned why I was out three nights a week having meetings with the fellowship or why at three o'clock in the morning I was on the phone for three hours. If I shook during the night her arm would wrap round my body and she'd ask me if I was all right. If we were out having dinner with our mates it would only take a nod across the table for her to know I was feeling uncomfortable and she'd make our excuses and leave.

Within days of her hanging up her clothes in my wardrobe, heaven knows how but the newspapers got wind of the story. Like all other press leaks in the past, it was probably someone close.

I didn't mind them having this particular story as I was happy. Let them write what they want, I thought, so I went about my business as usual. But Maria wasn't used to such scrutiny and has always resented being the focus of any attention whatsoever. When she used to take me to perform cabaret anywhere in the country the last thing she wanted to do was help me out on stage. There was no way I could get her to hand me props and prizes in front of an audience, so I had to make do with her passing things from the side of the stage. All that the audience could see of Maria was a hand coming out from behind a curtain, like a scene from *The Addams Family* movie.

On one occasion, whilst I was out shopping, Maria called me on my mobile to say that some newspaper men had come up the drive and were now peering in the house through the back window. When I asked her where she was exactly she told me she had dragged the phone from the kitchen and was hiding in the downstairs toilet.

I felt sorry for Maria. I'd put her through a lot and it still wasn't over. Everyone wanted a picture of Keith Chegwin's new girlfriend and, to this day, they still haven't got it. At present Maria is a blonde brunette whose father is a soldier, who used to be our nanny and is aged between 19 and 27. Not one of these 'facts' is true. And in the words of Maria, 'If they want to take my picture, think Claudia Schiffer! I'm no model, but I could do with the money.'

Now I made real contact with all my family again and invited them over for the weekend. Seven months previously I'd asked them to steer clear for a while and promised they'd see a new me on the other side.

We'd talked on the phone, but now I felt confident, knowing that I wasn't going to disappoint them. I looked forward, like a kid, to their arrival. They came all the way from Liverpool and London to see our new house and, hopefully, the new me. It was a joy to see them all. My brother Jeff and his little boy Hugo, my sister Janice, her partner Paul and their little boy Fred, and Mum and Dad all came to stay. It was like Christmas in the old days. It had been a long time since we'd had such a good time on our own.

Janice suggested that I get rid of all the old suits I had in the wardrobe and give them to my dad. I must have given him over twelve suits, ten shirts and more than fifty ties. They were suits from the past and, in one of the jacket pockets, Dad found an empty half bottle of whisky. Not for an instant did anyone think I'd hit the sauce again, but as usual they all took the piss and joked about how I was up to no good again!

The next four months went quickly and it wasn't long before I started work. During this period I continued with my AA meetings and savoured each one. For the first time ever I began to listen to other people and their day-to-day problems of steering clear of a drink. I began telling newcomers to the fellowship honestly how I was feeling and what I was going through.

Occasionally, the phone would ring at home and it was someone at the other end asking me for advice. I felt embarrassed that they thought of me as someone with tremendous knowledge and experience of living sober. After a time, I stopped giving out my phone number as it made me feel uneasy. For the time being, although I felt rather selfish, I decided to go back to keeping my own personal house in order.

Wherever I went it appeared that my every move was being watched. If I was having lunch in a restaurant, passers-by appeared to look at my glass on the table to see what was in it. If I ordered drinks from a bar, I could see the barman wondering what this alcoholic was going to have. I'd always leave my drink till last and took time looking at the soft drinks. I'd eventually order a mineral water with an ice cube and a slice of lemon. It was a stupid notion, but I thought that if I bought a coke, someone would think it was a Scotch and coke and get on to the tabloids. The same with apple juice, blackcurrant, dry ginger – they all looked suspicious. One cube of ice and a slice of lemon would hopefully be remembered by the barman if he was ever quizzed by a journalist.

I started to knock on doors for *The Big Breakfast* on 16 August 1993. In the beginning it was hard work, not physically but mentally. In treatment I'd been told how I'd lost a considerable part of my short term memory through excessive drinking. At the time it was difficult to believe one could lose so many memory cells but, sure enough, the clinic was right as always. Some days I couldn't even remember the town I was in or whose door I'd just knocked on. I'd have a total blank. I learned very quickly to make notes, writing down names, street numbers, and glance at them off camera if I got into trouble.

Although my short term memory appears to be shot to pieces, I know that over a period of time you can learn to develop your long term memory, so hopefully all is not lost. I have now got rid of my cards and I'm working on developing those skills. But there are still times when I have to ask people in the street to remind me where I am. They must think I'm mad.

By the time I started on *The Big Breakfast*, people thought that I'd overcome my alcoholism, all my problems had disappeared and that I was back on form. The Keith Chegwin of old, who smiled at everyone, was always on time and never let anyone down, was back. Personally I felt I wasn't quite out of the woods yet. Overcoming an addiction doesn't mean you can stop for a few months and it will all be over. It had taken a long time to come to terms with the fact that I was an alcoholic and I found it was taking me even longer to accept that I could never, ever drink again.

It was so easy to harp back to the days when I could make do with a couple of glasses of wine during a meal or the odd beer with my mates and leave it at that. But even now, nearly a year on, I had to keep reminding myself that I was a professional boozer who couldn't ever touch another drop. I was still only an arm's length away from a drink. One slip and all those instinctive old tricks would come flooding back. How to get drunk, where to get a drink and how to use alternatives if I could not get the drug of my choice. Each day was a real challenge, a new set of circumstances would arise and one slip could have sent me screaming back from whence I came.

Only recently I went cold when I was told about a friend of mine who, after four years of not drinking, went back to his alcoholic ways when he accepted a drink whilst away on holiday. Within days he was back on a drinking binge that lasted more than two weeks.

It's a dangerous game all alcoholics play, day in, day out. Drink is never out of the picture.

I went filming in Spain recently. The last time I was there was with Maria. This time I was on my own. I could have easily popped off to the bar for a drink, but I didn't. I confidently sailed through the ordeal and satisfied myself with my own knowledge that I didn't drink. I now appreciate that I don't have to impress other people by my efforts. I don't have to phone Maria or a best mate and tell them how good I've been. Nowadays, I get satisfaction from my own peace of mind and knowing that I haven't had a drink.

It doesn't stop me looking at other people at a hotel bar and wondering why am I an alcoholic and how come they are so different. We look the same, talk and walk the same, but when it comes to having a drink we are totally different. They can stop after a glass of wine, they leave a few dregs in the bottom or drink only one pint of beer. I often quiz close friends asking them how they do it. Not once have I been satisfied with their answers and as yet I've not heard one reasonable explanation. I don't think I ever will.

CHAPTER TWELVE

Since my appearance on *This Morning* I haven't had anything alcoholic to eat or drink. I steer clear of rum truffles and even wine gums. With the lifestyle I lead, I've found that eating out can sometimes be a nightmare. It's amazing how some of our greatest Cordon Bleu chefs find it difficult to create a meal without a drop of this and a touch of that to bring out that all-important flavour.

Being on the road and having to stay in hotels sometimes more than five nights a week I find the menu can be somewhat limiting for an alkie. Even when I'm invited to a friend's house for dinner, I enquire as to what is to be served. I feel like one of those boring vegetarians. I have to phone the host in advance and ask for my main course not to be *coq au vin* or a steak and ale pie.

I've been told that a lot of the alcohol disappears during preparation and cooking, but I prefer that it is not used in the first place. I just don't want to take the risk. I don't always tell my host that if the main course or pudding is soaked in booze I could be spending the next three weeks with them, as most people know about my drinking, but sometimes, for people who don't know me, I find it easier to tell them that I'm allergic to alcohol or that I'm on a course of tablets from the doctor and therefore I can't drink.

Some of my friends use the same excuse when questioned at a cocktail party or in the pub with a few mates after work. I found that I used enough excuses to get a drink, it's now even easier to make an excuse not to have one.

As time has worn on, I've stopped thinking about drink morning, noon and night. In the early days I was so full of self praise that if questioned about my last drink I could tell you for how many days, hours and minutes I'd abstained. Now it's a different story. I very rarely talk about it at home or in the presence of people I don't really know.

Occasionally a few people stop me in the street and tell me about their own drinking habits and enquire about how I gave up. I like to help those that ask by telling them a bit of my story and how I've managed to keep away from drink. There's no way I would ever suggest to them that they stop drinking but, on occasion, when I think they need that extra bit of help I tell them about how I found help flicking through the Yellow Pages and speaking to someone on the phone about my problem. There are loads of numbers available and there is always someone there to talk to at any time of the day or night.

In this sober life I now lead, I'm content that people feel free to drink in my company and may sometimes even get drunk. I'm often invited to the odd party as the evening's driver and many's the occasion I've given a helping hand to a friend as they've staggered to the car a little worse for wear.

If you were to knock on my door uninvited, don't expect a drink. I keep my house clean. But tell me you're coming, or come round for dinner and I'll make sure I get the drinks in. Mind you, on departure you can take the bottles home with you otherwise I'll pour them down the sink. I don't look twice at a mini bar now or live in fear of being first at the bar to order a drink. Mine is usually first and it could be anything from a blackcurrant and lemonade to an apple juice.

I don't worry if I stumble over the odd word, fall asleep on the sofa in the middle of the day or take a short cut through the drink section of a supermarket. If someone next to me smells of drink, I don't always walk away and worry whether other people think it's me. If I'm the loudest at the table during dinner, or the silent one at the end of the night, I couldn't give a toss. I know that I'm not drinking and I leave all the worrying for others to do.

Each day I take things as they come. I used to fret about work and social meetings. I'd sometimes pre-plan confrontations with people, at work and socially, weeks in advance. This used to lead to sleepless nights and feelings of anxiety. I remember one occasion when I had to confront a friend about some outstanding money. Weeks before I made the call I thought about what I should say. I even got up late in the night to make notes on how I should approach my friend. One morning when I'd built up enough courage to call him the post arrived with his cheque. All that pre-planning and preoccupation went straight out of the window and I'd lost a lot of sleep for nothing.

Only recently I had to say goodbye to someone who'd been handling my career for some time. It was not an easy decision to make. This time I thought it best not to make notes or spend sleepless nights planning my next move. I tackled him head on and was surprised at his reaction when I was thanked for my openness and honesty.

Having experienced life as a drunk and being used as a doormat, I find in sobriety that there are still those people from the old days who come back and try to do it again. Not this time, folks. I'm prepared to give as good as I get.

There was the odd story running round that I'd been seen coming out of one of my local shops with a full bottle of whisky. That I tried to hire a car and was turned away because I smelt of drink. I had also been seen in a local pub comatose on the floor and had to be carried out.

I was prepared for all this. Close friends had told me that they too had been subject to similar accusations in their early days of sobriety. But what do you do? Well, it's probably best to ignore this sort of malicious accusation, but I was happy to take it a stage further. To all those who accused me of drinking, I sent expensive solicitor's letters advising them that any more of these slanderous accusations would be dealt with through the courts where I would be after a considerable amount of compensation for such detrimental allegations.

The rumour got round locally that solicitor's letters were being sent to those who'd made such remarks. To this day, I've only heard one further drinking story relating to me. When I find the bastard who tells people that he knows my watering hole and has seen me drinking and drunk, I'll send Maria round for a friendly chat.

I was out shopping locally when I bumped into one person who had been a friend whilst I was drinking. He had a few of his mates with him and he desperately wanted to make them aware of the good relationship between himself and me, the guy from *The Big Breakfast*. He asked me about the show and joked about whether one morning I might be knocking on his door to surprise him. He said that only the day before he was passing my front door. Luckily, I timed it perfectly when I told him to keep passing.

I try not to be a vindictive person, but I do enjoy moments of triumph over some of those people who've gone around telling the world that I couldn't do it. 'Give him a couple of months and he'll be back on the bottle,' they said.

I went to the bank to draw some cash one day and tripped over on the way out. I was deeply embarrassed and my preoccupation for the next two days was with other people's thoughts and whether they'd think I'd had a drink. I have now stopped myself thinking about such trivial matters. I see people stumble all the time and I don't immediately think they've been at the sauce, so why should other people bother about me?

A lot of my initial concerns were all in my mind and the publicity I received about my problem didn't help as it exaggerated my own feelings for a long while. I have now learnt to deal with those as well.

I enjoy my job and the extra work that I do, but if it were to disappear off the TV screen tomorrow, it honestly wouldn't bother me. Life is much simpler now. I rarely attend film premieres, end-of-series parties or celebrity dos. I much prefer to spend time at home with Maria, Rose and Hollie. If I do go to the movies, I do so in my own time to watch something with action and adventure in it. You can't beat a tub of Hägen Daas ice cream, some popcorn, a coke and a good Arnold Schwarzenegger blockbuster.

In my drinking years, which I now reflect on, I had some wonderful times, too. Only in the heavy latter years were things so terrible. There were the good times when a few mates and myself would 'hit the town', go to discos and pubs and parties. I remember spending the night on someone's snooker table and having to walk more than a staggered mile home from a friend's wedding. I joined in mooning competitions at the local pub and spent nights with a good mate in my flat polishing off a bottle of brandy, talking about women and reminiscing about our school days. I remember fondly the times I spent studying *The World Atlas of Wine* and sampling wines from the best years that Bordeaux had to offer or how a wine buyer friend of mine would treat me to an evening of tasting. On one occasion I felt I was responsible for introducing a type of Lambrusco into his catalogue which went on sale to the public.

Close friends and work colleagues occasionally ask me whether I would drink again. I have to admit that there are still times when I wonder what it would be like to have a pint of lager or just one glass of red wine with a meal. This used to trouble me for a while. I thought there might be something underlying such wicked thoughts. Was I straying back to my old ways?

Having chatted to some of my friends with many years of sobreity, I have found out that they too often have similar thoughts. It's only natural for anyone to think what it would be like to drink again. But it's not the end of the world and I'm not having any sort of relapse. It's normal, even for an alcoholic, to have such curiosity.

One area of recovery that has taken me a long while to adjust to is focusing and concentrating on anything for any length of time. It's taken an age for my mind to centre on any matter concerning my future. I give the impression of having a carefree attitude to life, but there are times when I like to sit down and contemplate whether I'm doing the right thing. I look at my work schedule and wonder sometimes whether it's all too much for me to cope with. I am now an honest person and, for my own safety, I have to recognise the tell-tale signs that gave me such a horrific period the last time round. I am not prepared to let history ever repeat itself. Therefore, I am not afraid to let those around me know when I'm tired and under pressure. My employers know that I like to work hard, but that I always like to keep that little extra in reserve to help me scoop myself out of any dangerous situation.

I often hear people extolling the virtues of life without drink. At one time, I thought it was all bullshit, nice try, but it won't work for me. Well, I can tell you that life is good without that drink. I can still be the life and soul of the party, if I choose. I can still go to a club and enjoy it without a glass of vino in my hand.

Some of the more ardent non-drinkers will, like reformed smokers, tell you that their lives have been totally transformed. How business is booming and relationships have blossomed. Some have even told me that putting down the bottle brought them fame and fortune. Good for them, but that's not always the case. My story is somewhat unique. I consider myself to have been very lucky, but there are those who are not so lucky. For all alcoholics, life after putting down the glass can be an uphill struggle, but for some more than others.

If you stop drinking it won't always bring you fame or fortune. It won't keep some people out of jail or repair a marriage. But one thing I can promise you from first-hand experience is that it will stop you seeing the world through a quarter-inch piece of piping.

It'll stop you going round like the cartoon character Mr McGoo.

When I eventually gave up drink, I found that my lifestyle altered tremendously in all sorts of ways. I was forced, through not drinking, to open up my mind and think about my whole life and my future. In the early days, I thought there was precious little left. Naturally, I had my daughter Rose and Maria to love, a house and a dog to look after. But putting them aside, what else was there? The drink had gone and with it I thought there was no escapism, no easy high to take away my inhibitions, something I could relax with.

Professional counselling told me to take up a hobby, get active and even go to night school. But what they'd forgotten about was that for the fat, dull, uninteresting types like me this wasn't really an alternative. What could I do? How could I ever find something that would replace my bottle? The last thing I wanted was to go jogging or build an Airfix Fokker plane.

I basically decided to do what I wanted. I got out of bed when I felt like it, I spent time on my own when I wanted to and I went to meetings when I needed them. For over a year I spent most of my days doing my own thing. It was very selfish. Slowly but surely, I let others into my insular world. The times I spent indulging in my own thoughts grew less and I started to think about the rest of life as time moved on. During this period I naturally gave thought to my future and gradually took responsibility for it. My dream world that was so important to me appeared of its own accord. It came from the happy life I started to lead.

Sounds stupid, I know, but my smile came back. I started to laugh and have real fun with Rose and Maria. I began to get some real joy out of living. I became my old self without realising it. The Keith Chegwin that I once knew, who spent his time annoying friends with his practical jokes, came back at last. (Maybe they're not so grateful for that . . .) I took Rose on holiday for the first time since she was born. I had a brilliant time with her and Maria and I now have the memories to prove it.

I can now read a paper or magazine, listen to Radio 4 and, at last, do something which has been a major personal goal – write a book.

I didn't want to tell my story through someone else, a ghost writer who would have to compromise my account because of individual writing techniques. I wanted to have something of my own to remind me of the days when I drank. I sometimes flick through the original manuscript and think that only a few years ago I was incapable of taking on such a challenge. It may not be much to you, but being able to look back at the pages of this personal diary means a lot to me.

There are still tough times and life isn't all pie in the sky. Like everyone else, I have bills to pay, bank managers to please, a taxman and an employer to satisfy. But now, at last, I have a chance and a choice not to see it through the bottom of a glass or, more honestly, through the bottom of a bottle.

With special thanks to these few people to whom I'm forever indebted:

Maria and Rose
Mum, Dad, Janice and Jeff
Paul and Fred
Felix and Rue
Bob and Sue
Jim, Stuart and Bernard
Dave and Sarah
Pam and Ronnie
Steve and Bonnie
Rick and Lynn
John, Patsy and Tamsin
Ross
Tim and Mandy
My dustbinmen
Pat and Gerry
Lou Cummins
Val (from Princess Square)
Richard and Judy
Patrick Titley and Richard Maude
Nick Thomas and John Conway
Jim Brown
Bill Mason (for his kind words)
All my old mates at London Weekend:
Dougie Brown
Jeremy Ross Mawer
Dave Winslett
Mick Upton (thanks)
Planet 24, for trusting me
Ian, my hairdresser
To all those who took time to write to me and for their kind words.
. . . and finally, my wonder dog Hollie, for watching over me whilst I was drinking and sitting next to me whilst I was writing this book in the hope that I would have a fag break and throw her ball.

INDEX

Alcohol, effect on body 81
Alcoholics Anonymous 56, 81, 88, 107–8, 124, 135, 148
Alcoholism, KC's (in chronological order) 1–5
first drink 18
occasional glass of cider 26
drinking before performances 28
bottle of wine a day 34
liking for whisky 35–6
liking for sherry 37
no hangovers, 'in control' 37–8
dependence begins 38–9
blackouts 38–9, 42
heavy drinking all day 40
blackouts common 44
handling drink 45
speed of drinking 46
seeks information on drink problem 47–8
physical symptoms 47, 53–4, 62, 63
hiding bottles 49
throwing up 50, 74
not driving 50
bicycle trips for drink 50–1
drinking Night Nurse 52, 92
working and drinking 52–3
full alcoholism 53–4, 55
medical specialist 54–5
Alcoholics Anomymous 56
clinics for alcoholics 52

spell in 'Chesterton Grange' 59–86
more symptoms 62, 63
drugs 61, 62, 65–6, 72, 77, 81–2, 99
relaxation class 66–7
contact group 67–71
problem of celebrity status 71–2, 82
weight gain 73
interview 75–6
attends lecture 79–81
stories at group sessions 82
personal counsellor 83
sporting outing 84–5
leaves clinic 87
'dry drunk syndrome' 89, 90
thinking about drink 90
back on the drink 91–2
back to 'Chesterton Grange' 92–6
troublesome at the clinic 93–4
leaves the clinic again 96
pains in the rectum, and operation 97
living alone, rations drink 99
full drinking again 100, 101
visit to hydro 101–2
drunk at appearance in Torquay 102–3
back home, considers drinking important 104
working and drinking 104–9
after holiday, more drink 114

to another clinic 115
more drugs 115–16, 117
back to 'Chesterton Grange'
    116–21
expert on alcoholism 118–20
leaves 'Chesterton Grange'
    121
trying to cure himself 123–6
buys bottle, then binges 126–7
confesses truth on *This*
    Morning 129–31
the drive to stop 131–57
some friends desert him 134
meets many alcoholics 134–5
medical consequence of
    alcoholism 136
ubiquity of drink 145
sleeplessness 146
drinking now over 151–2
accusations still made 153
attitude now to drink 154–5
Allen, Janice 17
Alpen, Professor 75–6, 118
Angel, Mrs 24–5

Barbara Speake Stage School
    22–3
BBC, KC merchandising for
    138–9
The Big Breakfast 141, 142–3,
    148
Blackburn, Tony 28
Brown, Roger 83, 92, 93,
    118–19, 121
sees Maggie 94
advises KC on broken
    marriage 95
counselling 98–9, 123

Capes, Geoff 41
Channel Four
    The Big Breakfast 141–2
    The Word 139–41

Cheggers Plays Pop 27, 41, 44,
    88
Chegwin, Mr (father) 15, 17–18,
    19–20, 115
and KC's alcoholism 58, 104
visits by 99, 147
Chegwin, Mrs (mother) 15,
    17–18
and KC's alcoholism 58, 104
visits by 99, 147
Chegwin, Janice (sister) 15, 19,
    21
and KC's alcoholism 58, 112,
    116
partner Paul 58, 77, 83–4, 147
son Fred 147
visits by 77, 81, 83–4, 147,
    148
advice from 139–40
Chegwin, Jeff (brother) 15–16,
    17, 19
and stage 21, 22
at stage school 22–3, 24
in record industry 25, 29
visit from 147–8
son Hugo 147
Chegwin, Keith
see also separate heading:
    alcoholism
character
easy-going 88–9
joker 16
stage-struck 18–19
life (chronological)
birth in Liverpool, and
    schooldays 15–16
holidays 19–20
first appearance on stage 20
Happy Wanderers 21
more experience 21–2
film, *Egghead's Robot* 22
at stage school 22
television commercials 23–4

living with brother Jeff 25–6
miscellaneous work 26–7
singing with Kenny 26
Swap Shop 27
marriage to Maggie Philbin
    30
move to house in country 31
maria works in house 33–4,
    49, 56–8, 59
baby Rose 34–5
hard work 35, 73–4
charity work in Romania
    35–6
end of children's programmes
    40–1
pantomime 41–2
Star Search, talent show 42–4,
    45
expert on loos 50
mountain bike 50–1
Land Rover 57
first in clinic 59
visit from Maria to clinic
    71–2
computer games 72
thinks about television career
    73–4
interview in clinic 75
help to Kelvin 85–6
confident to leave clinic 86
loses Maria 87
possibility of living with
    Maria 95
buys cottage 98, 99
wish to write book 100
contacts Maria, moves to her
    parents 100–1
rumours in newspaper 101
work in Torquay 102
sees lawyer about divorce
    104–5
back home, sets listening
    devices 105–6

avoided by friends 106
appreciates dog Hollie 106
in pantomimes at Aldershot
    108, 136
holiday in Spain with Maria
    112–14
work 126, 136
accepts marriage to Maggie is
    over 136–7
relations with Maria 137–8
works in BBC merchandising
    138–9
presents pop quiz on *The
    Word* 139–41
help from Maria 140
does more television
    programmes 141, 142–3, 148
Maria moves in 146–7
contacts own family 147–8
poor short-term memory
    148–9
lifestyle 156
Chegwin, Rose (daughter) 4, 34,
    76
and the breakup 96
post-break 98, 101, 111, 126
future 137, 156
The Chegwins 21
'Chesterton Grange' 56–8, 59–86
    KC leaves 87
    KC returns 92–6
    KC leaves again 96
    visits 98–9
    KC returns 116–21
    drugs fewer 117
    KC leaves 121
    therapy meeting 125
Children's TV programmes 27–8,
    40
Clinics 56
Collins, June 22

Delirium tremens 73

Edmonds, Noel 27
Egghead's Robot (film) 22

Families of alcoholics 119–20
Fielden, Maria
  works in Chegwin household
    33–4, 49, 56–8, 59
  visits KC in clinic 71–2
  leaves the Chegwins 87
  later contacts 95, 100–1
  holiday in Spain with KC
    112–14
  more contact with KC 137–8,
    140
  moves in with KC 146–7
Finnigan, Judy 7, 11, 129, 130

Go Getters 141
The Good Old Bad Old Days 26
Granada Television see *This*
  Morning

Happy Wanderers Concert Party
  21
Hello magazine 133
Hulme, Anna 40–1

Jackson, Mr (talent scout) 20–1
Journalists
  search for KC's story 9–10,
    12, 82, 87, 111
  told of separation 111
  after *This Morning*
    appearance 131
Junior Show Time 21

Kenny (group) 26–7
Keynotes 106
King, Jonathan 29
Kinnear, Roy 22

Lamarr, Mark 140–1

McCartney, Paul, 15
Madeley, Richard 7, 11, 129, 130
Maria, *see* Fielden, Maria
Mame 23
Monkhouse, Bob 25

Newley, Anthony 26

O'Connor, Des, KC's
  impressions of 19, 20

Parsons, Charlie 141
The People false story 131
Philbin, Maggie (wife) 4
  television presenter 28, 29
  romance with KC 29–30
  marriage 30
  and KC's drinking 34, 39, 40
  baby Rose 34
  living in the country 36–7
  tired of KC's drinking 49
  tries to help 54–5
  sees KC in clinic 76
  receives KC back from clinic
    87, 88
  ends marriage 94–5
  after the break 98, 101, 104
  leaves with Rose 106
  announces separation to press
    111–12
  visits clinic 116, 119
  sees KC after his
    independence 125–6
  about KC's *This Morning*
    appearance 131
  KC accepts marriage over
    136–7
Psychiatric patients at the clinic
  77–8

Roache, Mrs, landlady 24
Rogers, Ginger 23
Romania, charity work in 35–6

Ross, Paul 141
Routledge, Patricia 22

Sky TV 42
Slattery, Tony 51
Star Search 42–4, 45
Sun newspaper 29, 82
Sunday Mirror 133
Swap Shop 27, 29, 44

Television commercials, as child
  23–4

This Morning, KC's appearance
  on 7–13, 126, 129–31

The Wackers 27
Wattis, Richard 22
Wilde, Jack 21–2
The Word 139–41

Yates, Jess 21